ENDORSEMENTS

I stand in awe of Brian Guerin's integrity, courage, and unwavering faith to believe God for the supernatural display of His manifest glory in the earth today. In my own life I have witnessed some of the most remarkable signs and wonders—uncommon, unusual, extraordinary works of God—but as the Bible promises, these heavenly manifestations will continue to increase in the last days. As I read *God of Wonders*, I was fascinated by the intriguing testimonies and glory stories that are contained within the pages of this must-read. Brian has experienced God's wonders firsthand, and he is ready to share them with you! This highly anointed book is also filled with practical applications and teachings that will enable you to live in this same realm of miraculous demonstration and will be enormously helpful for anyone who desires to go deeper into the things of the Spirit. Brian has prepared for you a revelatory road map that will lead you into greater realms of discovering God's presence, signs, and wonders in your own personal life. Get ready to read and be activated!

JOSHUA MILLS
Keynote conference speaker
Bestselling author, *31 Days to a Miracle Mindset*
Vancouver, Canada
Palm Springs, California
www.JoshuaMills.com

Brian Guerin is one of those unusual persons who has supernatural occurrences and manifestations visit his life and ministry because of the kindness of God and the grace of the Lord Jesus Christ.

Through his desire to know the person of God, he has been given a capacity to receive divine revelations that bring about visible manifestations of the presence of Jesus in the now.

As you read the pages of this book, your hunger for Jesus will be increased, your thirst for the spirit of God will be deepened, and your faith for God of Wonders will be sharpened to the place where you will be able to experience God in ways you never have before.

The revelation of the word that Brian shares will enable you to see, hear, and know Jesus to the place of holy satisfaction and glorious contentment.

As the Light of God shines upon your spirit and your soul, you will learn how to make Jesus known to others, bringing heaven to earth so that others can experience both the love and life of the living God.

Jesus said that unless you see signs and wonders, you will not believe. This "show me generation" must see signs, wonders, and miracles that are so profound in nature that they will be led to genuine repentance, sincere faith, and deep intimacy with the Lord Jesus.

Through *God of Wonders*, you will find information, inspiration, revelation, manifestation, and the ultimate glorification of the Lord Jesus.

In the book of Isaiah 60:1, it says, "Arise, shine, for your light has come, and the glory of the Lord has risen upon you. For behold, darkness shall cover the earth, and thick darkness the peoples; but the Lord will arise upon you, and his glory will be seen upon you." Dear follower of God, be prepared to enter into the light and the glory of God. As you read the pages of this book, may you know Jesus more intimately and manifest Him more evidently in your life and ministry. To God be the glory!

PASTOR TONY KEMP
President of Tony Kemp Ministries
and Embassy Christian Center
Hannibal, Missouri

To commune with and communicate God is the life-blood of our faith and the dispensation of the Spirit in which we live! This timely book is penned with simplicity, depth of insight, impartation, and stirs the hungry soul toward first love for Jesus. Brian walks in the speaking of God through "signs and wonders" like no other I know. His pursuit of God's Voice-Person-Presence, humility, and integrity are desperately needed in our generation, and a foreshadowing of what God is desiring to do on a global kingdom scale.

DAVID POPOVICI
Founding President of Kingdom Gospel Mission
Mediterranean Regional Impact

"He does great things past finding out, yes, wonders without number" (Job 9:10 NKJV). Jesus Christ is the greatest and ultimate Wonder. He has made Himself known, yet is shrouded in mystery. This is what keeps us coming to Him day after day, knowing Him and yearning to gaze upon the facets of His face we have yet to see. From the Wonder of wonders Himself, miracles and signs naturally flow. This is God's nature and it's awesome. Brian Guerin is one of the most intense Jesus lovers I know. Jesus is his food. He is convinced of this truth: "Jesus is the ultimate pursuit and highest revelation." Brian spends countless hours waiting on the voice of the Holy Spirit. This book will help you discover one of the beautiful ways in which He speaks and will continue to speak—signs and wonders.

Michael Koulianos
Founder of Jesus Image, www.JesusImage.tv
Author of *The Jesus Book*, www.TheJesusBookonline.com

There is nothing more wonderful than experiencing an incessant connection with Jesus Christ! From this place of intimacy the wonders of God's kingdom become a reality to those of us who really know Him. In this book, *God of Wonders*, Brian Guerin does an excellent job of providing a view into the realm of the supernatural derived through intimacy with the Lord! This view has been seen and lived out by many throughout the history of the church, as well as those who lived during Old Testament times. Brian not only details some of this important history, he also provides examples of God's glory and power still manifesting in this hour! If your heart longs to experience more of what God's kingdom has to offer you and if your heart motivation is pure in this desire, then I highly recommend this book!

KEITH COLLINS
Lead Pastor, FIRE Church, www.fire-church.org
Director, FIRE School of Ministry, www.fire-school.org
Founder, Generation Impact Ministries, www.keith-collins.org

GOD
OF
WONDERS

Angelic Wonder of Relational Guidance

While we're talking about an angelic wonder performed with coffee, here is another caffeinated sign of angelic assistance, on a much lighter note. This sign and wonder turned out to be not only very timely but life-changing as well. Many years ago, I was in a relationship with this very special young lady. At the time we were courting with the intent to lead toward marriage. With both of us having sincere hearts for ministry and very similar visions in life, you would have looked on the outside and assumed that this relationship was certainly meant to be. This being said, all both of us ultimately wanted was the divine will of God. And I have come to realize that, when hearing the voice of God with great precision, one should never look at the outside. God not only looks upon the heart of all matters, but also knows the future He has in store for each and every one. This is why James says:

> Come now, you who say, "Today or tomorrow we will
> go into such and such a town and spend a year there
> and trade and make a profit"—yet you do not know
> what tomorrow will bring. What is your life? For
> you are a mist that appears for a little time and then
> vanishes. Instead you ought to say, "If the Lord wills,
> we will live and do this or that" (James 4:13-15).

Angelic Sign: To Marry or Not to Marry

In this season of courting and a long-distance relationship, I found myself locked away one weekend in prayer, as I often love to do when the schedule permits. There is nothing like being with Jesus. I have come to learn in life that there is no higher fulfillment and no higher joy than that of merely being alone with Jesus one on

GOD
OF
WONDERS

EXPERIENCING GOD'S VOICE THROUGH
SIGNS, WONDERS AND MIRACLES

BRIAN GUERIN

DESTINY IMAGE® PUBLISHERS, INC.
P.O. Box 310, Shippensburg, PA 17257-0310
"Promoting Inspired Lives."

This book and all other Destiny Image, Revival Press, MercyPlace, Fresh Bread, Destiny Image Fiction, and Treasure House books are available at Christian bookstores and distributors worldwide.

For a U.S. bookstore nearest you, call 1-800-722-6774.
For more information on foreign distributors, call 717-532-3040.
Reach us on the Internet: www.destinyimage.com.

ISBN 13 TP: 978-0-7684-0425-8
ISBN 13 Ebook: 978-0-7684-0426-5

For Worldwide Distribution, Printed in the U.S.A.
1 2 3 4 5 6 7 8 / 18 17 16 15 14

DEDICATION

I dedicate this book to the greatest sign and wonder of all, Jesus Christ. You are the prize by whom I live. You are the reason for all that I do. You are the Love of my life. Please be glorified, I pray. Thank You for You, Lord Jesus.

I love You

supernatural deliveries of astonishing fruition. For whatever reason, these two instances both involved getting my resources to certain people. One was a delivery of my first authored book, titled *Modern Day Mysticism*, which has now gone out all over the world, producing great impact and impartation in many people's lives. We've heard testimony after testimony of the increase in dreams, visions, encounters, angelic activity, and signs and wonders breaking out in people's lives after reading that book. That is also my intent in writing this book, along with bringing increased wisdom and understanding about how God speaks and operates through the means of signs and wonders.

I was traveling through the beautiful mountains of Montana to minister at what was being called "The Gathering," and once. In reply, I casually asked from the other remote speaker, that they had received my books and were going to be ahead and place them on the book table. I thought, *What? Received my books?* I sent a text back saying, *What do you mean you received my books? I have my books with me.*

You see, I typically bring a box of books with me as a resource for people who I impart, and if they happen to sell out, at least people can preorder and get a copy that way as well. That's why I was really confused that this person apparently had my books too. Not only did I always carry them with me, but at the same time *Modern Day Mysticism* could only be obtained through the ministry.

So this person answered that they received a literal package delivery of my books, with my handwriting on it and everything. They thought, *Huh, I guess he wants me to bring these to the conference that we will both be speaking at.* The person also later told me that they wondered why on earth I would do that, as the cost of shipping the box of books would have been more than any profitable gains of selling the book anyway.

CONTENTS

INTRODUCTION

IN THIS BOOK I WILL NOT ONLY BE BRINGING GREAT ENLIGHTEN-
ment and teaching accompanied with countless firsthand accounts
of how God speaks to His creation through the performance of
signs and wonders, but at the same time releasing what I believe is
a very timely impartation for these same demonstrations to begin
breaking out within your very own life. I will be addressing four
of the main venues by which God performs signs and wonders
in order to communicate to His people. These four being atmospheric wonders, nature wonders, signs and wonders performed
by angels, and the pure manifestation of signs and wonders alone
being released from the presence and glory of God. I will also be
bringing great criteria and scriptural foundations for hearing His
voice through these methods of communication for the purpose of
hearing His warning, confirmation, exhortation, foreseen purpose,
and much more.

I carried on preaching the gospel, and lo and behold it wasn't more than a minute or two before I found myself back over in that same location. Suddenly, this ball of light about the size of a grapefruit manifested out of nudder and literally my right arm brushed me, and I immediately asked the crowd, "Did you see that?"

They instantly responded, "Yes, it was a light!" It had expected itself to the naked eye. You see the Bible speaks of the devil coming as an angel of light. "As" is the key word here, of course, meaning that he can only try to appear as a true angel of light, but he certainly is not one. The nugget to gather from this Scripture is that true angels are angels of light and it just so happens that they often manifest as light. James 1:17 also refers to God as the Father of light, which is another heavenly reference to what comes out of his wondrous glory—light.

Needless to say, this angel manifestation was an angelic wonder confirming the presence of the supernatural among us in that meeting. I just so happened to be discussing our generation's dire need for supernatural kingdom reality and heavenly encounters like never before. The faith in the meeting skyrocketed, as you can imagine. It's one thing to talk about the kingdom of God, the angelic realm, and supernatural encounters, but it is another thing when you see clear evidence that they are right there in your midst.

Seatbelt Ticket Disappearing Act

A quite funny angelic wonder manifested around a seatbelt ticket that I was issued at one point. Of all things that you would think of as grounds for an assisting angelic wonder, you certainly wouldn't not expect it to be a seatbelt ticket. But once again, this will show you how God is so loving and caring about the large, significant matters of life down to the very small, day-to-day activities and casualties of human error.

Chapter 1

INTRODUCTION TO SIGNS AND WONDERS

ALL THROUGHOUT THE AGES, THE ANCIENT OF DAYS HAS DEMONstrated His very nature, plan, and voice by way of communication through what Scripture refers to as "signs and wonders." I believe that we as believers are going to need ears to hear the voice of our Maker through signs and wonders, now more than ever. It states very clearly in Joel 2 that in the latter days there will be "signs" in the heavens and "wonders" in the earth; I am proposing these will be some of the most prolific means of communication between the God of heaven and humankind. I am also aware that the enemy will be hard at work in these last days in an attempt to bring great deception, and even a falling away of the elect, if possible: "For false christs and false prophets will arise and perform great signs and wonders, so as to lead astray, if possible, even the elect" (Matt. 24:24). You will notice that in times of God's moving and speaking, the enemy is always right there. He tries to copy the way God speaks, using the same manner but with an opposite purpose—to further the kingdom of darkness.

A great example of this is in the book of Exodus when Moses came before Pharaoh in order to set the captives free. We all know the story—Moses threw down his staff, which then transformed into a snake. The Lord had ordered him to do this as a "sign" that God was both *speaking through* him and had also sent him. Immediately, the sorcerers of Pharaoh began to perform the exact same sign. They threw down their staffs, which also became serpents, but Moses' staff swallowed them up, as light always triumphs over darkness.

The point being made here is that we as the Body of Christ, now more than ever, are going to need to clearly hear the voice of God, because communication by means of signs and wonders is going to escalate within our day and age like never before. Meanwhile, the enemy will be running a parallel display of false signs performed through false prophets in an attempt at mass deception. Although we will need to hear from God to avoid this deception, I do want to point out that the first and foremost priority is intimacy with God. We need to know how to hear God's voice through any means of communication simply because there is no higher goal in life than knowing Him. At the same time, it is imperative that we remain aware of how the father of lies attempts to mimic signs and wonders; he will use similar performances, seasons, and times, but with his own purposes, opposite to the kingdom of light.

What Are Signs? What Are Wonders?

You say, "Well, what exactly are signs and wonders?" They are twofold by implication. Signs and wonders carry both meaning and awe, revelation and fascination. We can define a *sign* as "an object, quality, or event whose presence or occurrence indicates the probable presence or occurrence of something else." In other words, a sign represents or points to the meaning of something else. According to this part of the meaning, God manifests *signs and wonders* to express a revelation. We could define *wonder* as "a feeling of surprise mingled with admiration, caused by something beautiful, unexpected, unfamiliar, or inexplicable." This second part of the two-part meaning of *signs and wonders* is the amazement side. As we see here, signs and wonders bring about two things. They carry a sincere depth of meaning, message, and revelation coupled with astonishment, amazement, and awe. This is a good starting point in gauging signs and wonders and their authenticity.

There are many things that happen throughout life that cause awe. There are many things that occur day to day that carry meaning. But the true signs and wonders directed from the throne will have both revelation and marvel intermingled as one. That is the amazing thing about God. I have never seen Him perform a wonder of any sort without an applied message, meaning, or purpose. There is absolutely nothing shallow about the King of kings. Every move He makes, every breath He takes is with great purpose and strategic intent. That is one thing you can be certain of, my friend— if He truly performs it, it is guaranteed to have sincere depth and meaning in manifestation and/or occurrence.

Reinforcement Factor of Signs and Wonders

I like to look at signs and wonders as reinforcement of the voice and nature of God. You see, my background is in overseeing the construction of custom homes. So I tend to look at many of life's circumstances through the filter of what I know well. And I tell you, out of all the intricate details and extensive craftsmanship that go into building a custom home, nothing is more important than the foundation. If you have a faulty foundation, I don't care how exquisite your finishing touches might be. When the foundation goes bad, everything else goes bad. Basically, as the foundation goes, so does the house. I like to look at God's being and voice through this lens. In construction, the foundation is made out of one of the most durable products ever created—concrete.

Concrete is one of the most dependable and impervious products known to man. But even a concrete foundation needs reinforcement. This typically consists of post tension cables, iron rebar, wire mesh, and more. These products add a bit of assistance to the foundation's overall strength and durability. Likewise, God uses signs and wonders to reinforce His voice and purpose in all of creation. His voice and will are plenty substantial in and of themselves. It's just that signs and wonders assist in strengthening and confirming the foundation of who He is and what message He's trying to get across. They affirm, approve, and authenticate His will. They certify, endorse, and appropriate His voice. Without a doubt, signs and wonders play a major role in God's communication with you and me.

"Mere Signs" versus Signs and Wonders

I also want to briefly point out, for the sake of understanding, the difference between signs alone and actual signs and wonders—which this book will mostly be referring to. There are signs that God will speak through in your life that are exclusively signs without the wonderment. Although these might not be technically categorized as a true *sign and wonder*, they still contain the voice of God. And they certainly have no lesser value. Examples of these signs apart from wonders would be God speaking through unique billboards, license plates, t-shirts, repetitive number correlations, newspaper headlines, receipt amounts, and so much more. As you can see, the sign has meaning we can apply without a supernatural manifestation of wonder to go with it. Although in this book I will be mainly addressing how God speaks through the fullness of signs and wonders, I do not want to minimize the significance of a sign alone. I have personally seen signs occur that far outweighed the accompanying signs and wonders, and of course vice versa. The point here is that we learn and grow in loving and knowing the voice of God, by whatever means and delivery it may come. That's what this whole thing called life is about—loving and knowing Him.

Needing a Sign to Believe

One thing I do want to get clear, right out of the gate, is the religious spirit of the Pharisee and Sadducee. These spirits are completely backward in how they relate to the operation of *signs and wonders.* They actually need or require a sign and wonder to believe. We see this clearly in Matthew:

> And the Pharisees and Sadducees came, and to test Him they asked Him to show them a sign from heaven. He answered them, "When it is evening, you say, 'It will be fair weather, for the sky is red.' And in the morning, 'It will be stormy today, for the sky is red and threatening.' You know how to interpret the appearance of the sky, but you cannot interpret the signs of the times. An evil and adulterous generation seeks for a sign, but no sign will be given to it except the sign of Jonah." So He left them and departed (Matthew 16:1-4).

If you approach God requiring a sign and wonder before you will believe in who He is or what He is trying to say, you can hang it up, my friend. You have better chances of winning the lottery. The Bible says very clearly in Hebrews 11:6 that we must approach God in faith, meaning that *faith* is the starting point in drawing near to

Him, not needing a sign to then produce the belief. The religious spirit of the Pharisee and Sadducee is completely backward, rooted in a place of doubt and seeking proof to correct the foundational problem of disbelief. God will never validate this type of behavior or even attempt to vindicate Himself to such a cowardly approach. Mark 16:17 says, "These signs shall *follow* them that believe" (KJV). Once again, it is very clear that the signs *follow* believing. Faith is always the access key to all things eternal. For all those Pharisaical know it all's who love to quote, "I won't believe it 'til I see it"— good luck. I pray one thing you do have alongside that disbelief is patience, because you never will.

Signs and Wonders in Scripture

Jesus Himself was the very demonstration of many signs and wonders, which were not even all captured biblically: "Now there are also many other things that Jesus did. Were every one of them to be written, I suppose that the world itself could not contain the books that would be written" (John 21:25).

This is the perfect time to discuss the common deception that, "Everything God does must be found in Scripture." I understand the good intention behind this belief—trying to protect oneself from being deceived by making sure that everything must be found in Scripture. But by believing everything must be found in Scripture, you can actually find yourself falling into deception and limiting what God can do through your own life. It is absurd to think that the God of all the universe and creation can be limited in His performance and deeds to one small, carved-out section of eternity compiled into one book. The Bible, on the other hand, is by all means the complete and all-sufficient source for salvation and walking out a relationship with God. But if you're going to actu-ally fall under the limited, deceptive mindset that everything God has done and will ever do by supernatural performance must be already recorded in Scripture, you are sadly mistaken, my friend.

The signs, wonders, and miraculous things Jesus did were not even all contained in the Bible. The deeper truth in discerning the things of God is not a matter of making sure that everything can be found in Scripture, but it's making sure that the signs you witness do not *contradict* Scripture. This is something He will *never* do.

Prayer

God, I thank You for Your authentic signs and wonders that display Your glorious voice. I thank You that we see because we believe, all out of our desire for an intimate relationship with You. As we move forward in Your many ways of performing these wonders, I pray that You would release a mighty impartation like never before upon each and every reader for this wondrous journey to begin.

have been clearly perceived, ever since the creation of the world, *in the things that have been made*" (Rom. 1:20). "In the things that have been made" are the key words to dwell upon here. You see here that an unseen God filled with countless invisible attributes is on full display for humankind to see, perceive, and understand through *that which has been made*. In other words, the invisible is continually speaking to us through the visible — namely, all of creation.

Impartation from a Nature Wonder

The first time I can remember beginning to realize that God will actually orchestrate nature around you in order to get a message across was back in late 2004.

Many people know of this account, as I not only wrote about it in my first book, but have also preached about this encounter all over the world. Leading up to this event, I had been in hard pursuit to encounter God. There was a stirring like no other to have a run-in with my Maker. I couldn't explain it or shake it away. I woke up with it deep inside me and went to bed with it late at night. Everything in me was crying out to have an encounter with God that would forever transform my destiny and call for His highest purpose and plan.

I was coming back from a conference driving a full-sized white Ford Expedition. I was heading from Dallas, Texas, where the conference had been held, back toward the Houston area. It seemed like just another ordinary day. I had worship music on, praying in unknown tongues while simultaneously worshiping the Lord. About halfway between Dallas and Houston, around 1:30 p.m., "suddenly" this great big falcon—about two feet high, with a wingspan of four to five feet—swooped down upon my car. It happened so fast and unexpectedly that I tried to swerve out of the way to miss the collision with this huge bird. As it swooped down upon

Chapter 2

ANGELIC WONDERS

ANGELIC WONDERS ARE SUPERNATURAL SIGNS AND WONDERS PER-
formed by God through His messengers, the angels. This is very
common in the protocol of heaven. It only makes sense that God
would use angels to perform these wonders as they are specifically
assigned to assist those who inherit salvation (see Heb. 1:14). They
are the very messengers of God's will to humankind and the ones
who assist us in performing it. If God has set up the function of
angels to assist us in fulfilling His will, then certainly they will
be heavily involved in the function of signs and wonders as well.
Again, signs and wonders are for carrying God's voice and message
to humanity. What are angels? God's messengers. So if God speaks
through signs and wonders—and this is what this whole book is all
about, learning to hear God's voice in the sign and His message in
the wonder—then certainly angels, who are messengers, will play a
big role in facilitating these wonders as well. I personally have probably seen more manifested wonders as a direct byproduct of angelic
involvement than any other means that I know. When dealing with

signs and wonders, you can be certain of this, my friend—angels are often the prerequisite by which they come into fruition.

Manna: The Bread of Angels

In the wilderness, the Israelites experienced one of the most fruitful wonders to date. God rained manna down out of heaven as provision for the children of Israel. I propose to you that angels were the facilitators who brought this manna to earth. If you read the Psalms, you will see manna referred to as the "bread of the angels" (Ps. 78:25). This implies that not only was this a supernatural substance of heavenly provision, but I also believe it was delivered by supernatural messengers—the angels. I also speak from my own experience, as I have not only had manna delivered to me directly by the angelic realm, but I have also had the great honor of seeing many more supernatural wonders manifest via angelic dispatch. Angels are far more often involved in the fulfillment of God's will within our lives than I think many of us are aware. Let's look at several other glorious wonders of God performed through His heavenly messengers.

Angelic Wonder of Gideon's Call

One of my favorite signs and wonders performed through an angel was with Gideon in Judges 6. Right after Gideon received his angelic commissioning as the mighty man of valor, he said, "If now I have found favor in your eyes, then *show me a sign* that it is you who speak with me" (Judg. 6:17). The angel proceeded to do just that. The angel of God said to him, "Take the meat and the unleavened cakes, and put them on this rock, and pour the broth over them" (Judg. 6:20). Gideon did so. Then, with the tip of the staff that was in his hand, the angel of the Lord touched the meat and the unleavened bread. Fire flared from the rock, consuming the meat and the bread, and the angel of the Lord disappeared (see Judg. 6:21).

That sign, performed by an angel, is what gave Gideon the confidence to tear down his own father's prized altar to Baal and build a new altar of righteousness, exalted to God. You see, signs and wonders are marvelous by nature. They produce great insight, confirmation, and surety in those trying to follow God to the best of their ability. They validate what God has already spoken to you about, approving His word and giving you a sense of certainty. Signs and wonders are like the stamp on the envelope that makes the message go forth. Often, you already have the message. You even have it all set for delivery. But until you receive the sign, or stamp if you will, the message cannot go forth. This is often the case when God uses signs and wonders to confirm what He has told you to do.

Peter's Multiple Wonders

Peter found himself in the middle of multiple angelic wonders, right when he needed them the most—when he was bound in jail. These supernatural performances were very simple. The meaning was within the operation. Freedom! In Acts 12, we find Peter chained up between two guards, waiting to be put on trial the day after Passover. It says an angel came in the night and struck Peter on the side, waking him, and at this his chains fell off.

Okay, stop right there. As if the chains just falling off at an angelic wake-up nudge wasn't astonishing enough, the guards didn't even wake up—the guards whom Peter was *chained to* and right smack in the middle of! Apparently, the angel already had them under some sort of comatose spell in order to free Peter. Peter then proceeded to follow the angel, thinking he was merely seeing a vision. What happens next? They walk right by the first and second guards! *What?* Say that again, please! How do you just walk right by not only one, but *two* sets of guards? It's easy when the angelic realm is involved, performing wondrous deeds of the heavenly kind!

I believe they were made invisible. Scripture clearly states, "sentries stood guard at the entrance" (Acts 12:6 NIV). If they *stood* guard, they certainly were not sleeping. This means Peter and the angel were made completely invisible and walked right by, unseen. If all of this isn't wild enough, next we see that the front gate opened on its own, allowing Peter's exit to complete freedom (see Acts 12:10). This is another profound truth that I have learned about the angelic realm. Angels can literally move objects around with no visible contact whatsoever. They will do this—as in this instance with Peter—to literally fulfill what God is trying to do; they will also move objects as a wonder in order to get across what God is trying to say. As far as I am concerned, I don't care what they do, move, adjust, or perform. Just speak, God, for Your servant is listening.

Angelic Food Service

We see an astounding wonder in First Kings, when Elijah is provided with supernatural food from an angel:

> And he lay down and slept under a broom tree. And behold, an angel touched him and said to him, "Arise and eat." And he looked, and behold, there was at his head a cake baked on hot stones and a jar of water. And he ate and drank and lay down again. And the angel of the Lord came again a second time and touched him and said, "Arise and eat, for the journey is too great

for you." And he arose and ate and drank, and went in
the strength of that food forty days and forty nights to
Horeb, the mount of God (1 Kings 19:5-8).

You see, my friend, there are some things in God's will for our lives that we simply cannot fulfill without angelic assistance. And one of those ever-so-needed functions, especially in this day and age, is none other than performing signs and wonders.

There have been many wondrous deeds done by angels—shutting the mouths of the lions in the book of Daniel, bringing strength to Jesus in the wilderness, opening the jailhouse doors in Acts 5, blinding the men of Sodom and Gomorrah, and the list goes on and on.

Angelic Wonders in Seattle

As I mentioned earlier, in my experience with signs and wonders, nine times out of ten their manifestations have been direct results of angelic involvement. You might not always know exactly where the sign originated from, but most likely the messengers of the celestial world were assisting somewhere along the way. This is also where dreams and visions come in very handy for understanding how God works. As I describe some of these experiences further, you will see how revelation functions in the wisdom of wonders.

Seen without Being Seen

One profound angelic wonder came about while I was ministering in the beautiful city of Seattle, Washington. It all started right out of the gate that morning, en route from Louisiana to Washington. The sun wasn't even up yet, as I had an early bird flight out of New Orleans, Louisiana around 6 a.m. I got to the airport, went through security, and stopped in a convenience store to grab a bottle of water before boarding the plane. I grabbed the water, approached the checkout counter, and then heard the cashier say to me, "Oh, welcome back," as if she had seen me before.

I had never seen the young lady before in my life. I said, "Welcome back? This is my first time in here."

She began to debate this with me, saying she had seen me come in that store a few minutes prior—same colored shirt and everything. I finally convinced her that she had not seen me and that this was my first time in the store, as I had just arrived. She still had this confused look on her face and asked, "Then do you have a brother who looks just like you or something?" I assured her that I did not, and we parted ways in some confusion.

Doing Only What You See the Father Doing

I then got on the plane and postured myself for prayer and adoration of His presence as we took off for Seattle, Washington. While basking in His presence, I was asking the Lord about the meeting where I would be ministering that evening in Seattle. I do this almost every time before I preach, wherever it may be. I have learned it is much more productive to do only what you see the Father doing—as Jesus did—than to follow any other method or agenda there is.

This whole thing boils down to love and obedience. If you can't obey, you have no business putting your hand to the plow. The kingdom life is very simple. You spend all of your first and foremost priorities on loving and knowing Him. Then, out of that place, you simply obey what He has told you to do. I have also learned that you must lose the spirit of pleasing man when you take on this life of doing only what He tells you to do, because quite often He will ask you to do things that either make no sense to the natural mind or are clearly not the direction other people desire you to go. But the Bible says very clearly that the carnal mind cannot understand the things of the spirit, so what do you have to lose other than popularity? I'd rather be popular in heaven for the sake of His glory any day of the week. So love and obey, and you'll do just fine.

In prayer, I saw a vision of the Anaheim Angels' logo before my eyes very clearly. I could see the large, red capital letter A with an angel's halo around it while the whole logo itself was leaning to the right. I knew immediately that the Lord wanted me to speak on and release an impartation of angelic assistance from the kingdom of God. I saw a few more details about the meeting and most importantly knew what basic direction the Lord wanted me to go in.

After seeing this vision, I began to realize some of what was going on with the lady "already seeing me" in the airport convenience store. Our angels can appear just like us in the natural, whether physically to the naked eye or even in dreams and visions. This was a key nugget that the disciples understood in the book of Acts. When Peter was freed from jail and knocked on the door where the saints were praying for his deliverance, Rhoda, in opening the door, had more faith that she would see Peter's angel than Peter himself, standing right before her eyes. The disciples were not only familiar with the angelic realm in everyday life, but they also had this insightful revelation that an individual's personal angels often take on the exact personification of their heavenly assignment.

Having had prior experience in this, I was well aware that this cashier lady very likely could have seen my angel going before me, as I had also been praying in the spirit for the entire drive to the airport that morning. Prayer and worship are like the welcoming committee for the angelic realm, by the way. I also want to point out quickly the difference between this and bilocation. Many times, for various kingdom purposes, people are seen in separate locations from where they physically are at the moment. But what many people don't know is that often they are seeing this person's angel, not an actual duplicate of the person. This is where bilocation gets mistaken for what is actually that person's angel, sent to forerun or minister and assist in diverse purposes. There are, however, true bilocations, which are a very real happening and another kingdom protocol.

Manifestations around the Message

Continuing on, as if the incident at the airport wasn't enough, when the plane landed I got up to get my luggage from the overhead compartment. Lo and behold, my compartment was already wide open, waiting for me to just grab my luggage. I thought, *How'd the stewardess not catch that?* Yet I also understood that the angels were at it again.

I don't know if you fly much or not, but an open compartment *never* happens. The plane always lands with all overhead compartments tightly shut. This is what the pilot calls a "landing check"—the flight attendants check everyone's seat belts, make sure tray tables are securely fastened, and last but not least, they close all the overhead compartments. I am positive that the angel waited until just before we taxied to the gate terminal to open the compartment. The flight attendant not only made sure all compartments were shut, but she just so happened to be sitting catty-corner across from my seat while we safely landed. Just in case, I stood up to get my bag and looked all the way down the shell of the plane—yep! My overhead compartment was the only one opened, thanks to the kindly assistance of angelic hosts.

You might say, "Well, why did an angel need to open the compartment merely for you to grab your luggage? Couldn't you have just opened it yourself?" Yes, of course, but realize that often the very thing God desires you to minister on will also manifest itself to confirm the message that needs to be released. This is another way God speaks in order to get His point across. In this case, it was the involvement and assistance of angelic messengers. So now, as you can imagine, there was no question in my mind as to what He wanted me to minister on—not after this barrage of angelic activity accompanied by a vision, all happening within a span of several hours leading up to the service.

Angels Winning in Seattle

While still in worship before getting up to preach, I had this random thought: *Why did God speak to me about releasing the angelic realm to assist kingdom purposes by way of the Anaheim Angels' logo?* I mean, there are so many different ways He could have shown me or spoken to me in order to get His point across. So I checked the Internet on my phone while still in worship to see what was the big deal with the Anaheim Angels. What do you know! They were playing that very night in Seattle, Washington! The exact location where our service was being held! I then knew what was going on, as I have seen God do this time and time again. He is really amazing in His ways of communication and actually quite fun. If you don't get stuck in a religious box, you will find out that God speaks through anything and everything you will allow Him. He is simply too vast for any one form or method. And He loves to speak parallel with natural events in the region when they carry implications to what He is saying. We just need ears to hear and an obedient heart to follow, letting Him do the rest.

Discovering that the Angels were playing in the Seattle as a natural sign of what God wanted to do, I realized that they would win as a further confirmation of triumphant angelic release in that region. I knew they would win because when I saw the logo it was leaning into the right. When I see things either by vision or dream and they are facing to the right, this always speaks of victory in the natural and something being "right" or correct. When something is facing left, it speaks of defeat and something or the decision being "not right," because it is left and incorrect. Begin to pay attention to this now, because once you know that God speaks in this way, He will begin to use this method of communication in your own life.

I preached on the angelic realm and told everyone about the soon-to-be-victorious Angels playing that night in the city in conjunction with the vision, and sure enough, they won. They were actually playing at the same time as our service was going on.

Hidden Riches and Angelic Wonder

One interesting thing happened, though, in the fruition of the meeting. As I was preaching on the angelic realm and how angels operate in assisting the Body of Christ, I began to drift off into what I call the topic of "hidden riches." It is supernatural provision that comes solely from heaven: "I will give thee the treasures of darkness, and hidden riches of secret places, that thou mayest know that I, the Lord, which call thee by thy name, am the God of Israel" (Isa. 45:3 KJV). The New Testament parallel would be when Jesus commanded Peter to cast his line in the sea and pull up the first fish he caught. And what was in the fish's mouth? A coin, or "hidden riches," to the exact amount of their temple taxes (see Matt. 17:24-27). There are many other biblical examples of this, like the quail feeding Elijah or the oil overflowing the widow's jars. Hidden riches are basically when your source of provision is solely God, and God alone leads you to treasures in secret places to provide for your needs.

In continuing the sermon, I began to realize that what seemed like a sidetrack in the message could very well be Holy Spirit guidance. So I had everyone lift their hands as we prayed for supernatural provision and the fulfillment of Isaiah 45:3, the hidden riches. Closing the meeting, I also released an impartation of the angelic realm, which was the initial assignment. The very next morning I was scheduled to speak again, and a lady came up to testify in the meeting of a profound angelic wonder. She began to share with us how, the night before, she and some of her friends from the conference went back to their hotel room, discussing the meeting and the things of God. As they were conversing after the service and the Angels' victory in Seattle, she unzipped her purse to grab something. To her utter amazement, she found a huge white feather resting on her wallet! It was a profound angelic wonder that directly coincided with the message about receiving angelic assistance intertwined with supernatural provision! (See fig. A in Appendix.)

I love it when God does this. As I mentioned earlier, not only will God begin to manifest the very thing He wants you to minister on, but more often than not the manifestations will also follow the releasing of the word. This is part of what the Bible is talking about when it mentions signs and wonders *following* those who believe (see Mark 16:17 NKJV). So in this case, the feather represented the angelic realm and an increase of angelic assistance in this precious woman's life. The feather resting upon her wallet was a sign of provision coming soon by supernatural means, as Isaiah 45:3 promises. Needless to say, we saw quite an array of angelic events that day, intermingled with His glorious wonders.

Angelic Wonder of Airport Protocol

I tell you what, while we are talking about angelic activity in an airport, here is another recent incident that was quite fun. This will again show God's concern with assisting us even in the small, seemingly-mundane details of daily life.

A dear friend of mine, Ryan, and I were getting ready to fly out to the beautiful Dominican Republic. We were going through check–in, just like any other day. "May I see your ID?" the airline agent asked.

"Sure," I replied, handing her my passport.

"You can put you bag on the scale, sir," she said. On the scale it went.

One small detail I forgot to mention—I had weighed my bag back at the house as I always do before leaving on trips. I was trying to keep the bag under 50 pounds, because you are looking at paying a $100 fee for anything over that. Oh boy, it weighed 52-odd pounds. I thought, *Oh well. I guess I will have to just take some stuff out and shift it to my carry-on when I get to the airport if they don't let me by.*

So, back to the airport. My luggage was resting upon the scale, and my fingers were crossed. Shoot! It weighed right around 52 pounds. Ryan and I both saw the scale. I waited for the lady to either say, "Pay up," or "Remove the weight." Then, there it was! An angelic wonder like I had never seen before! Ryan and I both saw with our very own eyes as the scale began to drop weight, as if somebody was lifting the bag ever so gently. Would you believe the scale went all the way back to exactly 50.0 pounds? Fifty pounds exactly! I looked at Ryan immediately and said, "Did you see that?"

He said, "Of course I did!" We even took a picture of this wonder in utter astonishment. Needless to say, we headed to the gate, ready to board with no extra fees and a light carry-on. As minor as it may seem, angelic wonders can come in some of the most handy circumstances, leaving you with nothing but pure gratitude and thanksgiving. (See fig. B in Appendix.)

Angelic Sign of Coming Judgment

The morning of May 10, 2010 I was in prayer. About midway through, I looked over and noticed that my coffee mug had been moved. I was seriously taken aback, realizing that the very coffee mug I had been drinking out of had been supernaturally repositioned. Not only was that surprising, but even more astonishing was that it had been propped up on my ceiling fan control. It was almost to the point of tipping over, coffee still in it. I'll get into the meaning of this sign in a minute. (See fig. C in Appendix.)

I don't know how angels do it, but they can move objects around right in front of you without you even being aware of their movement. I believe they supernaturally transport items at times from one place to another. There was one time when an angel literally removed the armrest covers of a chair right out from underneath my arms without me even knowing it. I was sitting in this chair in prayer and never even knew it happened until I went to get up from prayer and saw both armrest covers tucked neatly into each other down on the floor by my feet. (See fig. D in Appendix.)

The angel did this as a sign and wonder for me not to rest my arms during that weekend in prayer, because there was a battle going on. This specific weekend of prayer paralleled the time when Moses was not allowed to rest his arms during Israel's battle against the Amalekites.

> And so it was, when Moses held up his hand, that Israel prevailed; and when he let down his hand, Amalek prevailed. But Moses' hands became heavy; so they took a stone and put it under him, and he sat on it. And Aaron and Hur supported his hands, one on one side, and the other on the other side; and his hands were steady until the going down of the sun. So Joshua defeated Amalek and his people with the edge of the sword (Exodus 17:11-13 NKJV).

It was crucial that Moses' arms stay up in intercession, so when his arms grew weary, Aaron and Hur assisted in keeping them up. Similarly, that weekend I was being commissioned to pray.

Back to the coffee mug incident. I immediately knew that an angel was behind the movement of this coffee mug; now I was left to discover the revelation behind this. Soon enough, I realized that this was a parallel to Jeremiah 1:13, where God asks Jeremiah, "What else do you see?" Jeremiah answers, "I see a pot boiling in the north, and it is about to tip over this way" (Jer. 1:13 GNT). God goes on to explain that this represents a coming judgment about to be tipped over and poured out due to national sin. This angel was making the same sign through the positioning of my coffee mug about to tip over. Realizing this, I thought, *Well, why did this angel prop the coffee mug up on my ceiling fan control?* You must remember—everything done from heaven is extremely detailed and strategic. We must pay close attention and search out the meaning in everything God says and does. It is similar to looking for hidden treasure, at times. If you don't pay close attention, you might just walk right by the riches that are tucked away. Without a diligent search, you might very well miss out on the value and worth that was there for you to discover.

Pay Close Attention to Heaven

Now back to my question concerning the coffee mug propped up specifically on my ceiling fan control. There was some precise reason behind using this object alone. After all, I did have my Bible and other books there on my nightstand, which the angel very well could have used for this Jeremiah 1:13 tipping effect. I then realized that this would be the very process through which judgment would be poured out. A control for a ceiling fan controls none other than the ceiling fan itself. What do ceiling fans produce? Whirling winds. This judgment would be poured out—due to national sin, as mentioned in Jeremiah 1—in the form of tornado winds of mass destruction.

The very next day, the news was filled with the previous evening's disaster. That same evening of May 10, 2010 witnessed a tornado outbreak of historic proportions. Over sixty tornados touched down, affecting large areas of Oklahoma, Kansas, and Missouri. Damage was estimated to be over $595 million in central Oklahoma alone. This was the second largest tornado outbreak in Oklahoma's history; the first being the major outbreak of 1999 in which over seventy-four tornados reportedly touched down.

When natural catastrophes come upon a nation at historic levels, it might be wise to consider the cause. Regardless of what your theology may be—whether you think God is behind the judgments, or God doesn't judge anymore, or God's hand of protection is forcefully removed due to our disobedience—that is not the point here. The point here is that sin draws judgment within the earth. The wages of sin is death.

It is a very clear in Scripture. We must pray for our city, for our state, and for our nation. Second Chronicles dictates God's prescription for revival:

> If my people who are called by my name humble themselves, and pray and seek my face and turn from their wicked ways, then I will hear from heaven and will forgive their sin and heal their land (2 Chronicles 7:14).

God is calling us to turn our hearts back to God, as He would much rather fulfill Jeremiah 29:11 for us, "For I know the plans I have for you, declares the Lord, plans for welfare and not for evil, to give you a future and a hope." This is the promise of the loving Father whom we serve.

Angelic Wonder of Relational Guidance

While we're talking about an angelic wonder performed with coffee, here is another caffeinated sign of angelic assistance, on a much lighter note. This sign and wonder turned out to be not only very timely but life-changing as well. Many years ago, I was in a relationship with this very special young lady. At the time we were courting with the intent to lead toward marriage. With both of us having sincere hearts for ministry and very similar visions in life, you would have looked on the outside and assumed that this relationship was certainly meant to be. This being said, all both of us ultimately wanted was the divine will of God. And I have come to realize that, when hearing the voice of God with great precision, one should never look at the outside. God not only looks upon the heart of all matters, but also knows the future He has in store for each and every one. This is why James says:

> Come now, you who say, "Today or tomorrow we will go into such and such a town and spend a year there and trade and make a profit"—yet you do not know what tomorrow will bring. What is your life? For you are a mist that appears for a little time and then vanishes. Instead you ought to say, "If the Lord wills, we will live and do this or that" (James 4:13-15).

Angelic Sign: To Marry or Not to Marry

In this season of courting and a long-distance relationship, I found myself locked away one weekend in prayer, as I often love to do when the schedule permits. There is nothing like being with Jesus. I have come to learn in life that there is no higher fulfillment and no higher joy than that of merely being alone with Jesus one on one. To bask in His presence and be consumed in His voice is truly unmatchable to anything this life can provide.

So there I was, just soaring in the presence of His glory that day. I can even remember a certain shift about midday when the presence of God became very strong and overwhelming. After coming out of that thick presence, I just so happened to look over at my coffee mug that I had left on top of my chest of drawers, and something was different. The coffee stirrer that I used to stir the creamer into the coffee had been pulled out of the mug and ever so gently rested upon the top of the mug. The stirrer was now lying horizontally across the rim of the coffee cup. I knew immediately that the angelic realm was up to something.

As I mentioned earlier, angels will purposefully shift objects around as a wonder, and if you pay close enough attention you will hear the voice in the sign. As I looked closer, I noticed that the stirrer was pointing directly at the young lady with whom I was in courtship. You see, I just so happened to have a framed picture of her with her friend upon that chest of drawers, and the coffee stirrer was now pointing directly at her in this framed photo. (See fig. E in Appendix.)

I had no idea what this was supposed to mean, so I just left the now-performed sign right in its place until I could figure it out.

Investigate the Wonder

I want to point out that this is very key when interpreting signs and wonders. You always want to pay attention to every detail possible in their manifested surroundings. Where did they happen? What time did they happen? How did they happen? What were you doing, meditating upon, or discussing when it happened? Basically, you are doing a full investigation of the associated sign. The Bible says in Proverbs, "It is the glory of God to conceal things, but the glory of kings is to search things out" (Prov. 25:2). Like it or not, my friend, the kingdom of God is just this way. God spoke to the prophets in riddles, while Jesus spoke in parables. When it comes to the kingdom, only the hungry will eat and the seekers will find. God's voice and will for all of eternity is far too valuable to just be lying out in the wide open somewhere for any passerby to find. Like anything else in life that is of great worth, it will cost you, my friend, to follow and heed the voice of your Maker.

Coffee Cup of Love

In looking further into the surrounding details of this now manifested wonder, I noticed one major detail. The cup that I happened to be drinking coffee out of that day was given to me by this same young lady. It was given to me on Valentine's Day as we both shared loving gifts, commemorating not only our relationship but also the holiday at hand. So as you can imagine, this cup was red and white with hearts and love of every kind written all over it. This cup was clearly a representation of love.

Now, the stirrer pulled out of the cup and pointed directly at her. I was aware that this sign and wonder obviously had something to do with our relationship at the time and love. Leaving the mug in its exact position overnight, because I was still not sure what this could mean, I woke up the next day and looked again. To my utter amazement, the coffee creamer had separated from the coffee and rested on top in the form of a heart with wings. If I didn't already know that an angel was involved in performing this supernatural sign about love, the creamer had now formed a heart with wings. (See fig. F in Appendix.)

It was almost as if the angel was leaving his signature or something. Looking back, this precious woman of God and I are very thankful, because marriage is not something you want to play around with. This is your second highest decision in life, after following Jesus. If there is any time you want to make sure you are hearing His will clearly, it would be when choosing your spouse, with whom you will spend the rest of your life. Finally! The light bulb went off! What the Lord was trying to say became clear.

I thought, *What do stirrers do?* They stir and mix two things together as one, which would have represented marriage—the two becoming one—and all this within the context of what the coffee mug represented—love. So pulling the stirrer out would obviously represent the opposite of marital merging. Not only would it represent the opposite in separating the two, this literally happened the very next morning when the creamer separated from the coffee, forming a heart sign accompanied by wings—an angelic autograph. Also, don't forget that the stirrer was pointing precisely at her to confirm that this sign pertained specifically to our relationship.

Additionally, the Lord spoke to me very clearly that this whole thing hinged off of Scripture repeated three times in the book Song of Solomon, "*do not stir* up or awaken love" (see Song of Sol. 2:7; 3:5; 8:4 NKJV). I love how He does this. Only God can think up things like this. Who on earth thinks to give a sign of relational separation with a stirrer from a coffee cup of love, alongside the command of "not stirring love" from one of the most intimate books in the Bible? Nobody. Only God. Needless to say, this dear woman of God and I were very thankful for His voice in this matter sparing us from moving toward marriage, because neither of us wanted to pursue a course outside of His perfect will.

Supernatural Deliveries

In discussing angelic signs and wonders, I have come to realize that angels are quite amazing—not only at delivering messages, but actual packages too. On two separate occasions, angels were behind supernatural deliveries of astonishing fruition. For whatever reason, these two instances both involved getting my resources to certain people. One was a delivery of my first authored book, titled *Modern Day Mysticism,* which has now gone out all over the world, producing great impact and impartation in many people's lives. We've heard testimony after testimony of the increase in dreams, visions, encounters, angelic activity, and signs and wonders breaking out in people's lives after reading that book. That is also my intent in writing this book, along with bringing increased wisdom and understanding upon how God speaks and operates through the means of signs and wonders.

I was traveling through the beautiful mountains of Montana to minister at what was being called "The Glory Conference." En route, I received a text from the other keynote speaker that they had received my books and were going to go ahead and place them on the book table. I thought, *What? Received my books?* I sent a text back saying, *What do you mean you received my books? I have my books with me.*

You see, I typically bring a box of books with me as a resource for people when I travel, and if they happen to sell out, at least people can go online and get a copy that way as well. That's why I was really confused that this person apparently had my books too. Not only did I always carry them with me, but at the same time *Modern Day Mysticism* could only be obtained through the ministry.

So this person answered that they received a literal package delivery of my books, with my handwriting on it and everything. They thought, *Huh? I guess he wants me to bring them to the conference that we will both be speaking at.* The person also later told me that they wondered why on earth I would do that, as the cost of shipping the box of books would have been more than any profitable gains of selling the book anyway.

As I arrived and we were discussing this matter in detail, the pastor's wife walked up and said, "You wouldn't believe it, but the exact number of books you sent was the exact number of people who preordered the book from before." It all started to make sense now. Although I certainly had nothing to do with the delivery of the books, it met a specific kingdom need. What happened was, I had ministered at this same church before and had already sold out of books, so that many people were not able to get *Modern Day Mysticism*. So the pastor had set up an order list of those who wanted to purchase the book and did not get to, for the next time I come to town. Well, would you believe that the exact number of people on that list was the number of books shipped to this speaker through angelic coordination?

I was speechless. Not only were the people who wanted the book from before taken care of, but I also had my standard shipment of books for those who wanted the book at this conference as well. God is something else at times. It was so funny how long this other speaker and I went on and on in debate. "You sent this box to me."

"No, I didn't. Why would I do that when I brought a whole box of books with me?"

"But your handwriting was on the box!"

"I don't know how! I not only didn't send the box, but I never even saw it."

When we finally figured out that there was supernatural involvement behind this assignment, everything started to make sense. This person tried to go home and find this box for me, as this would have been one of my prized memories, but apparently had misplaced it or thrown it away. Needless to say, I have now learned that not only can angels appear like you, as I mentioned before, but they can also mimic your very own handwriting. I love how God cares about each and every one without missing out on any details. Especially when it comes to getting His message and kingdom out there to a generation. You will find out that He is very jealous for the gospel and adamant in getting the message out. This is also why I believe this next occurrence also made sure a resource of kingdom purpose was assigned and sent forth by angelic delivery.

Steward the Mysteries

There is a journal that the Lord had me compile not too long ago titled *Steward the Mysteries: Journaling God*. It is based out of First Corinthians 4:1 where Paul calls us to regard ourselves as *stewards of the mysteries* of God. It is all about stewarding God's voice and nature throughout life for the purpose of knowing Him and fulfilling your highest destiny and goal. A dear friend of mine in ministry ordered a copy one day, and this is how the wonder began. You see, the journal is a bit different from my first book, *Modern Day Mysticism*. The book is sent out all over the world from our home ministry office, whereas the journal is sent directly from the printing distributor. We have a bulk quantity of *Modern Day Mysticism* stocked and waiting at the office in MDM, and I actually personally sign each copy that leaves the door.

The *Steward the Mysteries* journal is a bit different. Each individual copy is printed out unit by unit per request to the printing distributor, which then ships them directly to the customer, and we never see or handle the copies. Needless to say, this per-unit printing process on top of shipping out to be received typically takes anywhere from five to ten days. I'll never forget the day a dear friend in ministry placed an order. Not only was I notified by email of the online purchase, but this friend also texted me excited to receive the new resource. I, of course, responded with equal excitement for what God had in store for them. Lo and behold, two days after the order had been placed, I got a text from the person with a picture attached to the text. It was a picture of them holding the journal in hand and stating how excited they were to have received it as they were going on a ministry television show that night. This person was asking me if they could bring the journal on the show to further emphasize to the need for *stewarding God's voice*. I responded, "Of course, that's a great idea!" while thinking, *How on earth did you get the journal already?* This was impossible! Typically the journal does not even leave the printing distributor for up to three to five days after the printing is complete, much less arrive somewhere at an alarming rate of only two days from the purchase date. Again, I realized that in order to meet the need for kingdom resources, angelic assistance had gotten involved once again.

Ball of Light

Another profound wonder of angelic involvement happened in this meeting where I was ministering when this supernatural light manifested in midair. This has happened on many occasions where orbs of light, rays of light, beams of light, and flashes of light will supernaturally appear when angels are present. In this particular meeting, I stepped off of the platform as I typically do—I like to walk around as I preach. This specific night I found myself talking about the supernatural realities of heaven and how our generation must see a demonstration of the gospel we preach. I began to walk over near the right side of the room and this loud frequency vibration began to resound through the monitors of the sound system, right when I would step into that area with the microphone. So I hurried up and stepped away from that location and mentioned to the people that an angel was probably standing there. I was sort of joking to the congregation, yet I knew that this frequency vibration could very well be due to an angel standing there.

I carried on preaching the gospel, and lo and behold it wasn't more than a minute or two before I found myself back over in that same location. Suddenly, this ball of light about the size of a grapefruit manifested out of midair and flew by my right side. It startled me, and I immediately asked the crowd, "Did you see that?"

They instantly responded, "Yes, it was a light!" It had exposed itself to the naked eye. You see, the Bible speaks of the devil coming *as* an angel of light. "As" is the key word here, of course, meaning that he can only try to appear as a true angel of light, but he certainly is not one. The nugget to gather from this Scripture is that true angels are angels of light and it just so happens that they often manifest as light. James 1:17 also refers to God as the Father of lights, which is another heavenly indicator of what can come out of His wondrous glory—lights.

Needless to say, this light manifestation was an angelic wonder confirming the presence of the supernatural among us in that meeting. I just so happened to be discussing our generation's dire need for supernatural kingdom results and heavenly encounters like never before. The faith in the meeting skyrocketed, as you can imagine. It is one thing to talk about the kingdom of God, the angelic realm, and supernatural encounters, but it is another thing when you see clear evidence that they are right there in your midst.

Seatbelt Ticket Disappearing Act

A quite funny angelic wonder manifested around a seatbelt ticket that I was issued at one point. Of all things that you would think of as grounds for an assisting angelic wonder, you certainly wouldn't not expect it to be a seatbelt ticket. But once again, this will show you how God is so loving and caring about the large, significant matters of life down to the very small, day-to-day activities and casualties of human error.

I was in prayer one morning when I heard in the spirit, clear as day, "Click it or ticket." I thought, *Oh, no!* I knew immediately what this meant, as this is a very common phrase the police force uses to advertise the importance of wearing your seatbelt. I have to admit, I'm not the best at remembering to wear seatbelts—besides, I can't stand them. I call them wrinkle belts, as all they seem to do is put these huge wrinkles in your freshly pressed shirts. But nevertheless, the Bible says we are to abide by the law of the land, and I not only firmly believe in wearing them but also strongly advise everyone to do so.

That being said, I prayed, "Oh God, please help me to remember to wear my seatbelt, as You are clearly trying to warn me of an upcoming ticket." Would you believe that not a week later, there it was—a seatbelt trap? The cops were waiting around a hidden corner, giving out seatbelt tickets. Prior to this, I hadn't had a seatbelt ticket in forever and a day. Was I wearing my seatbelt this day? Of course not. I pulled over and the ticket was issued. I thought, *Oh Lord, I'm so sorry. You tried to warn me and I still messed the whole thing up.*

A number of days passed and I made my way downtown to be a good citizen and pay the seatbelt ticket. I went up to the front desk with my issued ticket in hand, with the cop's signature and mine on it as well. I handed it to the lady and she headed to the files to look up the ticket so that I might pay it and be on my way. She looked and looked and looked. She asked me my name again. She then said, "And how exactly do you spell your name again?" as she continued to look. After her thorough search, she came back up to the front desk and said, "Sorry sir, but this ticket is nowhere in our files. I can't find it anywhere."

I said, "But here it is," pointing to the physical ticket in hand that I was issued as I insisted on paying the ticket.

She said, "Sorry sir, without the copy of the ticket on file we can't receive payment, nor does it go on your record."

As I went on about my day, I thought, *What on earth? How strange was that?* I did have a subtle awareness that this could have very well been orchestrated by heaven. After all, He did try to warn me of the incident that certainly did come to pass. Quite some time passed, and I had honestly forgotten all about not only getting the ticket but the strange event downtown when I tried to pay it off.

I was in prayer one morning when I got taken into this vision. In the vision I was walking right up to the counter where you go to pay off seatbelt tickets. It was the same exact counter that I had been to in the natural. In this vision, I walked up to pay for my ticket, just the same. There was an angel behind the counter in the form of very sweet elderly lady. She was fiddling through the books where the tickets were supposed to be filed—the exact place where my document should have been in the natural. In the vision, I began to tell this angel/lady my name to help find my ticket on file that I might pay it. She stopped me and said, "I know your name. I'm here to help you." Then I came out of the vision.

I was flabbergasted. I now knew for sure that heaven was behind the misplacement of that ticket. This vision was God merely confirming what had already taken place. This angel in the form of a precious, sweet-natured lady not only obviously knew my name, but was also there to help me. What better way to describe the assignment of angels? That is exactly what they do. Help people. Needless to say, God did it once again. He performed an astounding wonder through angelic assistance that even followed my shortcoming and error. I tell you, He's a gracious God full of compassion and mercy. At the same time, I want to point out that this is not a free license to live a compromised life. We must never take for granted the price that Jesus paid for us in making this grace complete. Obey in all things, with all you are, and when you make a mistake or fall short or miss the mark, praise God for His loving-kindness and move forward in pleasing Him.

Angelic Wonders of Healing

Another one of my favorite signs and wonders that angels perform is directly tied in with healings and miracles. I have learned over the years that angels will actually tap you, nudge you, or brush you in exact body parts before you step into meetings to preach, signifying which precise physical needs for miraculous healing are going to be answered. I've seen this happen time and time again. I've seen this with deaf ears being opened, lungs being healed, barren wombs made alive, and so much more. The point here is that angelic beings are involved in God's purposes within the earth across the board. Many think that they are mere messengers alone. They certainly are that, but I would say "facilitators of heaven" would be a much more apt title. They get involved in just about every aspect of heavenly function, and we must realize this comes with eternal purposes. So next time you are about to go minister somewhere—or even if you're not in "ministry" and are about to step out into the marketplace—do not be surprised in the least if you are tapped, nudged, or brushed by angelic intuition, pointing you toward someone's dire need and an upcoming miracle.

Angelic Oil Confirmation

Speaking of angels performing wonders through bringing physical attention to the human body, here is an astounding occasion where a similar sign unfolded. I was ministering at this church where we were seeing wonders of all sorts break out. But this one particular wonder was quite peculiar. Before service, I lay down for a brief power nap, as I like to do at times to recharge. As I was just about to fall asleep, an angel grabbed my right arm and lifted it in the air as I heard, "Jehoiakim," in the spirit.

To make a long story short, Jehoiakim was a king who began to reign in power at the age of 25, and the meaning of his name just so happens to be "the Lord has set you up." So I knew by the spirit that the Lord had someone, age 25, who was going to be in that meeting. The Lord wanted to give his life a new level of kingly anointing and power, and he would also represent a release and corporate word for that body at large. I also knew that the angel lifting my right hand represented the verse, "The Lord's *right hand is lifted high*; the Lord's right hand has done mighty things!" (Ps. 118:16 NIV). This would directly tie in with the mighty right hand of the Lord, lifted in support of the new reigning power of Jehoiakim coming upon this house.

The service began and I released the word. Sure enough, the 25-year-old I was looking for came forward. With hands laid on, the power of God rushed upon this young man mightily. I also simultaneously released what I knew to be the corporate word for that body—coming into a new reigning kingship and authority, parallel to Jehoiakim and the Lord's mighty exalted right hand.

The very next morning, I was in the pre-service prayer room of this church. I personally feel this is the most important room in any church, by the way, as the real shift of all things eternal happens in the secret place and in prayer, not behind the pulpit. All that ministry culminates in is the walking out of that which has already been accessed through prayer. So in the prayer room, there it was—a full on manifestation of supernatural oil. And where of all places? The *right armrest* of the prayer room couch. This was clearly the sign following the released word and the angel lifting my *right arm* in parallel with the *right arm* of the Lord from Psalm 118:16. The new oil and anointing of authority and Jehoiakim kingship was coming upon this corporate body. (See fig. G in Appendix.)

There are so many more instances of angels performing signs and wonders that it would just boggle most human intellect and reason. At the start of writing this chapter, I began to get gold dust upon my hands—the realm of glory, assisted by the angelic, was conveying His voice. I share this in setting the atmosphere of faith around you and unveiling how common these realms are to be in each and every believer's life.

Prayer

God, we thank You for the angelic realm assisting in Your mighty wonders. Release them, I pray, to do Your divine protocol, assisting humankind in this destined journey of knowing and loving You. Let them ascend and descend for Your wondrous display even now on each, I pray.

Chapter 3

NATURE WONDERS

IN THIS CHAPTER WE WILL BE GOING OVER THE MANY WAYS THAT God performs signs and wonders throughout the realm of nature. We will see how God actually orchestrates and speaks through the very surroundings of life as we know it. My prayer for you as you read this chapter is that not only will these wonders of God's ongoing communication begin to break out within your own life, but that you may also gain a whole new sensitivity to God's voice and better receive the frequency at which God speaks. God is communicating many things through the earth around us, but until we have the correct receptor to pick up on that communication, these messages don't get through. Just as an airplane is in need of a runway, a radio needs frequency, the Internet needs bandwidth, and microphones need speakers. It is the same with humankind hearing God. We must align ourselves as high-quality recipients to retrieve and hear His voice.

One of my favorite verses in the Bible that describes God speaking through nature and His creation is found in Romans, "For His invisible attributes, namely, his eternal power and divine nature, have been clearly perceived, ever since the creation of the world, *in the things that have been made*" (Rom. 1:20). "In the things that have been made" are the key words to dwell upon here. You see here that an unseen God filled with countless invisible attributes is on full display for humankind to see, perceive, and understand through *that which has been made.* In other words, the Invisible is continually speaking to us through the visible—namely, all of creation.

Impartation from a Nature Wonder

The first time I can remember beginning to realize that God will actually orchestrate nature around you in order to get a message across was back in late 2004.

Many people know of this account, as I not only wrote about it in my first book, but have also preached about this encounter all over the world. Leading up to this event, I had been in hard pursuit to encounter God. There was a stirring like no other to have a run-in with my Maker. I couldn't explain it or shake it away. I woke up with it deep inside me and went to bed with it late at night. Everything in me was crying out to have an encounter with God that would forever transform my destiny and call for His highest purpose and plan.

I was coming back from a conference driving a full-sized white Ford Expedition. I was heading from Dallas, Texas, where the conference had been held, back toward the Houston area. It seemed like just another ordinary day. I had worship music on, praying in unknown tongues while simultaneously worshiping the Lord. About halfway between Dallas and Houston, around 1:30 p.m., "suddenly" this great big falcon—about two feet high, with a wingspan of four to five feet—swooped down upon my car. It happened so fast and unexpectedly that I tried to swerve out of the way to miss the collision with this huge bird. As it swooped down upon the car, it spread its wingspan to full length, gazing through the glass directly into my eyes.

This falcon's eyes stared right through the windshield glass, straight into mine—eye to eye. As I tried to swerve the car out of the way, I could just imagine this huge falcon coming through the windshield, as I was going around 75 miles per hour on the highway. I imagined the bird crashing, glass shattering everywhere, and then a dead falcon to deal with. Swerving off the side of the road but then quickly back on to the highway, I was startled yet grateful that no other cars were around.

Immediately, I looked in my rear view mirror to check for a dead falcon rolling on the street. I thought, *Surely, at least I caught one of his wings with the fender of my car*. But the bird wasn't there. I quickly looked through my side view mirrors—nothing there.

Then, I looked back up into the air, hoping to see him flying off, as I was out in the open flatland of Texas. The bird was nowhere to be found.

To this day, I don't know if this was an angelic being that took on the appearance of a falcon, or a real falcon that God had His hand upon to initiate this encounter. But what I do know is that ever since that experience with the falcon swooping into my life with fully-spread wings and his piercing eyes looking directly into mine, I have not been able to shut off the realm of the prophetic. Eyes to see in the spirit have been a direct result. This encounter is where it all began for me concerning dreams, visions, and trances.

If you look up the falcon family, you will find one common theme among them all—eyesight of pin-point precision. It was a week or so later that I went into a prophetic dream of this man foretelling soon-coming death, which would come to pass five years down the road.

Visions and dreams began to flood into my life as the Lord would teach me the interpretation. I would be shown many events before they took place, either literally or by parable. I then began to see into upcoming governmental events and be foreshown natural catastrophes in specific regions and locations. Foreseeing worldwide events has now resulted from this one encounter with one falcon on the backside of nowhere—in the flatlands of Texas.

Nature Wonders in Scripture

All throughout Scripture you will see God performing signs and wonders through nature in loving communication and to fulfill His purposes.

Right out of the gate, we see in the book of Genesis where God used a dove to perform a sign with Noah after 40 days of flooding. God allowed Noah to send the dove out time and time again until the dove retrieved an olive branch and returned to Noah as a *sign* that the flood waters had receded.

Another famous account in the Bible where God performed a sign and wonder through nature is in Numbers 22. This is the story of Balaam and his talking donkey. There are two astounding details to pay attention to in this event. Not only did God perform a supernatural exploit by way of an animal communicating with Balaam, but many fail to realize that this same donkey had its eyes opened to the realm of the spirit and was able to see the angel with the drawn sword. Out of these two supernatural gifts from God, I actually believe the ability to see in the spirit was the greater of the two. Had God not opened this donkey's eyes to the angel with the drawn sword, he would have continued along the path right into the Balaam's certain death. We see here that God once again communicated through a sign and wonder, sparing Balaam's life through nature. Why didn't God just open

Balaam's spiritual sight to see the angel with the drawn sword against him? Why didn't God just tell Balaam what was lying in wait in the path ahead, instead of opening the donkey's eyes and going out of His way to have the mule supernaturally communicate with Balaam? Because this is what God does—He performs signs and wonders through various means to get His point across, generation after generation.

One of my favorite signs and wonders ever performed by God through nature was when Abraham was about to sacrifice Isaac. God supernaturally provided a ram in the thicket right at the precise moment of Abraham bringing down the knife to end his precious son's life. The timing of this event is absolutely remarkable. It blows my mind every time I think about it. Every second of every minute of every hour passed by that day, as Abraham cut the wood for the altar, rounded up his son, climbed the mountain, built the altar, and bound his son to the altar as the sacrifice. The timing went all the way down to the last second, right before plunging the knife into his very own treasured, God-promised son. Lo and behold! At the very last second, a ram appeared in the thicket! Praise God forevermore! Timely indeed! One would have better chances winning the lottery than the odds of that ram appearing in a nearby thicket at that very instant. Once again, a profound exploit performed through nature by God Almighty, forever faithful and true.

Another profound wonder in nature actually performed by the Son of God was when the disciples were in need of supernatural provision. The collectors of the temple tax had come and were looking for their dues. Jesus thought, *Easy enough*, and He told the disciples to go cast a hook into the sea. He then said, "Pull up the first fish you hook, and in its mouth you will find a coin worth enough for my Temple tax and yours. Take it and pay them our taxes" (Matt. 17:27 GNT). Once again, the God of wonders comes through indeed.

To mention a few more biblical occurrences of God working wonders through nature, Jonah and the whale was nothing less than spectacular, even to the point where Jesus referred to Jonah being in the belly of the whale for three days and three nights as a sign parallel with His death and resurrection.

Another astounding wonder fulfilled through nature was when Jesus cursed the fig tree as a sign of judgment upon bearing no fruit. The very next day the disciples found the fig tree dead all the way down to the roots (see Matt. 21:18-22).

There are also the accounts where God used nature to bring plagues against Pharaoh for the hardening of his heart. In Exodus, time and time again wonders in nature were performed against Pharaoh in judgmental plagues. God used frogs, gnats, flies, and even locust (see Exod. 8–10).

We also see—as crazy and hard to fully grasp as this account is—how bears were used to play out Elisha's curse upon these hecklers who came against the prophet of God (see 2 Kings 2:19-25).

Needless to say, God repeatedly performed signs and wonders through His very own creation—nature. I will now share some of the many personal experiences I have had over the years of God moving and speaking in this very same manner. I pray above all that these experiences would not only enlighten you to how God communicates and works through wonders in nature, but I also release these same occurrences within your own life for the purpose of intimately knowing Him more.

Parallel of the Praying Mantis

Many years ago, the Lord took me into a season of intense prayer and seeking His face. This season lasted for right around a year to a year and a half. I would seek the Lord for no less than nine hours a day, seven days a week. Often when my schedule permitted I would be in His presence for up to 12, 14, and even 16 hours at time. There was a supernatural grace like never before to just be with Him. I was only requiring around four to five hours of sleep per night at this time. It was like I was literally living off of the life and virtue that proceeded from the throne. This season of pursuit contributed to much of what I see and operate in today in life and ministry. There was so much opened up to me concerning His voice, presence, and kingdom during this span that only eternity will tell all that was deposited, released, and imparted at that time.

Early in this window of pursuit that the Lord had sovereignly called me into, I began to notice this praying mantis that would come appear on my back porch time and time again. For months he would come just sit on my back porch in prayer posture, as praying mantises do. Often I would find him sitting on the back of my chair. I'm no rocket scientist by any means, but I had an inner knowing/inclination that this praying mantis could very well be a sign of some sort. This point in time was still quite early in my days of experiencing signs and wonders, which I now know to be very common ways God speaks.

The praying mantis continued to come and show up on my back porch in his precious little prayer posture and look at me with those buggy eyes. He became my little buddy for the time being, and I even ended up taking pictures and video of my praying little friend. I then was intrigued and began to look up the praying mantis by way of an online encyclopedia. To my surprise, I found out that the actual origin of the name *praying mantis* means praying prophet! I couldn't believe it! God was sending a parallel sign in nature to coincide with the season of prayer that He had me in, as well as the joint call of a prophet that I was already aware of. Not long after I realized the meaning within this sign, the praying mantis appeared no more.

I have come to realize something about how God performs signs and wonders, which I would like to point out. This is absolutely imperative in learning how to hear His voice in the sign and realize how He operates within the function of the sign. Most often, if there is an authentic sign and wonder being displayed within your life from God to you, this sign will continue to manifest until you get the meaning of the sign. God is so good and loving and considerate and patient in everything He does. He will gladly go out of His way to perform a supernatural display of a sign or wonder over and over again until He knows that you have understood what He is trying to say. I thank God for this, as many times I wasn't the sharpest tack in the box if you know what I'm saying. I needed His patient yet continual pursuit of me to know what He was trying to say. You will notice that when you have come to fully understand the message at hand, the sign and wonder will stop. This is a good thing. Do not be concerned. This is often merely because you have understood the message.

One other time a praying mantis showed up like this was when I and five other dear friends in ministry went away to a prayer cabin to lock up for several days in prayer. We try to do this annually to hear the voice of God for the upcoming year. This weekend of postured prayer brought about the return of the wondrous sign of the praying mantis.

I Send You Out Amongst Wolves

Another case of God's amazing signs and wonders through nature was astounding indeed, not to mention quite timely.

It was just another day as I knew it in my home town of Baton Rouge, Louisiana. I was driving down the road while talking to my best friend in life and ministry, David Popovici. He is the founder of Kingdom Gospel Mission, which is a profound apostolic ministry within the region of modern-day Mesopotamia.

Of all things, he began to tell me how God was speaking to him that very morning out of Matthew 10:16 where Jesus says, "Behold, I am sending you out as sheep in the midst of wolves, so be wise as serpents and innocent as doves." I had also been taken into a vision that very same morning where I saw both his and my newsletters, and was told that we would be maligned. So needless to say, we were very excited for what was to come. (I'm teasing.) But still, we were grateful as we broke down what God was obviously trying to get across, while at the same time we tried to heed the warning of opposition to come.

As David continued discussing how Jesus was sending us out among wolves, literally right before my very eyes a wolf ran out into the street across the road, dead in front of my truck, in broad daylight! I immediately asked David, "What time is it?" as I checked my truck clock simultaneously to make sure one of us had the accurate time.

I have come to learn over the years that when God performs any kind of sign or wonder that one of the main revelations behind why He does it is hidden in the time. He is a stickler when it comes to timing, numbers, and dates. You must always check the time of the manifested wonder if you want to keep up with what God is doing and saying for what reason and why.

Lo and behold, the exact time at which this wolf ran out in front of my truck was 10:16. There it was, a nature wonder once again. God had orchestrated this wolf—which, by the way, is the first one I've ever seen in real life before or since—to run out at the exact hour and minute of the chapter and verse which David and I were discussing. "Behold, I am sending you out as sheep in the midst of wolves, so be wise as serpents and innocent as doves" (Matt. 10:16).

Sure enough, the opposition followed like clockwork. It was no longer than a week or two later that I began to be publicly maligned and falsely accused, as my vision had foreshowed. David also began to go through multiple stages of resistance on many fronts. The revelation that God had been speaking to us both—on top of the emphasis brought to the matter by the nature wonder—assisted us greatly in overcoming the enemy's plan of attack.

This is another great purpose for God performing signs and wonders. They are often a confirmation of what He has already spoken to you about.

Battle of the Angels=Revelation Made Known

Another profound sign and wonder performed through nature was in correlation with a Daniel fast that I was in, upon God's direction and plan.

The Daniel fast, mentioned in Daniel chapters 1 and 10, is a very special fast that tends to bring about great understanding and revelation. You will notice that in Daniel 1 when Daniel entered this type of fast—which basically consists of vegetables and water— he was given insight into all kinds of literature, and even given understanding into all sorts of dreams and visions. In Daniel 10 he entered another fast of the same manner for three straight weeks. What was the end result of the fast? Revelation. Gabriel appeared to Daniel and stated, "I have come to make you understand what will happen" (Dan. 10:14 NKJV). Needless to say, this fast is absolutely imperative to operate at a high level of understanding, revelation, and insight into all matters of life.

Just about every Daniel fast I enter typically brings about parallel wonders and visions of profound insight and revelation. But this particular Daniel fast brought about a nature wonder that I will certainly never forget. I was nearing the end of this three-week fast in correlation with Daniel 10:2-3. Driving down a very common city road one morning, all of a sudden this falcon swooped out of nowhere toward my left and began flying alongside my truck. This huge bird was flying probably seven feet off the ground right out in front of my truck near the left front fender. He was flying so abnormally close while soaring parallel with my truck that it was obvious something supernatural or God-orchestrated was behind this. The thing that made this incident all the more crazy was that this huge falcon was also carrying a long, beheaded black snake within its claws. It was as if this bird was intentionally flying this close and so low to the ground to make sure my attention was caught and that I could see this beheaded snake. It was as if this bird was showing off this beheaded snake to me like it was a prized trophy or something. The nature of this account was so wild and up close and personal that it felt like I was living in the Discovery Channel.

After what seemed like a lifetime of this paranormal exhibition of nature, the falcon swooped up into a nearby tree and just sat there on victorious display. (See fig. H in Appendix.)

I thought, *What on earth was that all about?* Later, I realized that this was without a doubt directly tied in to the Daniel fast that I was concluding. You will notice in Daniel 10 that Daniel was in fasting and prayer for three weeks. At the end of the fast, Gabriel appeared to him to make known the revelation at hand. It is important to note what Gabriel says—during the three-week interval, there was a battle going on in the heavens. It was directly connected to Daniel's fast and the valuable revelation he needed. The forces of darkness wanted to stop the revelation from being made known to humankind, while archangels Gabriel and Michael were en route to deliver that very same message. That being said,

Daniel's fast was literally empowering forces of light to bring forth the revelation of God to that generation. You will never fully know what is at stake in eternity concerning angels, demons, and the fulfillment of God's will, but you are playing a direct role concerning its coming to pass.

As you search into this supernatural event, things become clearer and clearer. One of my favorite Scriptures in all of the Bible is Proverbs 25:2: "It is the glory of God to conceal things, but the glory of kings is to search things out." I have learned over the years that seeking and searching leads to great discoveries in the kingdom of God. The majority of the time God speaks through parables and hidden meanings, and if we aren't willing to search them out we will miss out on the intended message at hand. This is also why Jesus often spoke in parables, so that the average listener would not grasp what was really being said from God to man.

You might say, "Well, if God really loved us, wouldn't He make it plain?" I tell you it is because He loves you that He does not make it plain. The Bible says that the hungry shall be filled, and that He is a rewarder of those who diligently seek Him. He does this on purpose so that you will seek after Him and find Him as the ultimate goal. He is also very aware that in pursuing and searching out His voice you will be running into the very nature of who He is, time and time again. This in turn makes His very likeness and nature flourish within your life.

You see, you can only become like something or someone you hang around. It is absolutely impossible to be influenced by someone with whom you have had no contact. This is the secret behind why God set up this system of seeking and searching to discover His voice and plan. If we could just read steps one through twelve on how to walk out the perfect Christian life, we would no longer need Him, His presence, the Holy Spirit, or any other means of communication for that matter. Thereby negating life's highest purpose of all—relationship with the God of one true love; the Author and Finisher of our faith; He who was, and is, and is to come; the God of perfect wisdom, grace, and mercy divine. You see, as we seek Him and the knowledge of His voice, we literally take on the very attributes of God. We become the very thing that He intended from the beginning—the reflection and image of Himself. That is why I am very hesitant to link up with, rely upon, or covenant with those who do not pursue and search out a true, intimate relationship with God. It is absolutely impossible to reflect that which you have not been in contact with.

Abide, my friends, like never before. Reside with Him, I say—it is of the utmost necessity. Pursue the God of one true love. You will never regret this. Throw away your self-help methods and human efforts of bettering life as you know it. You become what you seek and discover what you find. There is no greater way to become like God than to spend time with Him alone. You will always reflect that which you behold. Pursue, abide, love, and dwell.

Light Always Wins

In getting back to the falcon account with the beheaded black snake, the Lord showed me that this wonder in nature was an exact parallel with the account from Daniel 10. You will notice that Daniel 10 is one of the most paramount Scriptures in all of the Bible for highlighting the battle that goes on between light and darkness. We are literally given an account where archangels and regional princes of darkness went head to head in battle, directly hinged upon the fasting of Daniel and the revelation at hand. Needless to say, archangels Gabriel and Michael overcame due to Daniel's persistence in remaining in the fast for 21 days.

When Gabriel reached Daniel, he mentioned that Daniel's prayer was heard on day one, but the fulfillment was hindered for 21 days in the realm of the spirit because of the opposing principalities of darkness. The Lord began to break down this nature wonder for me one detail at a time. The falcon I was shown represented the angelic realm, and the beheaded snake was, of course, the opposing forces of darkness at hand. The Lord was speaking to me as I concluded the Daniel fast, saying that the forces of darkness had just been overcome by the angels of light. Revelation could now come, and it certainly did. That same morning and the following it was like the heavens were opened with crystal clear insight, understanding, and great revelatory flow. The battle was won, and the revelation was made known.

Often we forget that the enemy is the author of confusion and misunderstanding. He loves to hinder the voice and presence of God by any means possible. The Bible even mentions how the devil blinds the minds of the unbelievers. He is a professional at what he does, but so is God. While demons seek to hinder, blind, and dull our senses, angels are hard at work to bring about the fruition and fullness of God's will for all of humankind. They bring clarity, understanding, wisdom, and virtue. I challenge you, while in fasting and prayer—remain diligent, my friend, as you never know what is being held up in the heavens and what heavenly treasure is waiting to be released to you on the other end of each and every costly venture.

Address of the Angels

In concluding this account, there is one last detail that will blow your mind. As if this live "Discovery Channel" experience were not enough of a parallel to Daniel 10 and the fast that I was in, there is one last detail that put the icing on the cake. This will again reveal to you not only how detailed God is in everything He does, but how strategic He is in every wonder He performs. This is why I can't stress enough how we must steward His voice and mysteries alike. First Corinthians 4:1 calls us to be "stewards of the mysteries of God," and we must do just that or we will continually miss out not only on the intimate relationship which He intends to have with each and every one of us, but the fulfillment of His highest purpose for life through destiny divine.

I not only parked and took pictures of this victorious falcon overcoming forces of darkness as he flew up into a nearby tree, but I began to check the location of the street that this paranormal event occurred. Lo and behold! I couldn't believe it! The actual address where the falcon precisely swooped out to then fly alongside with his victorious trophy in hand was 10021 Angels! (See fig. I in Appendix.)

Mind-boggling was an understatement, as you can imagine. God tied in the exact numbers out of Gabriel's mouth to Daniel regarding the fast being heard and victoriously completed on day 1 through 21 in the address of 10021. At the same time, He chose the home of the "Angels," tied to the most prolific Scripture in all of the Bible where angels are the focal point of the battle at hand. I love how He does what He does! He never ceases to amaze me time and time again. As if the wild nature sign I had just experienced was not enough, the confirming message was sealed and delivered in the precise location at the address of 10021 Angels. Only God can pull off these kinds of events—the God of all creation, all knowing and true.

The Turtle of the Tarrying Promise

In continuing with these wonders of God's voice in nature, let me share another profound instance when God used a turtle, of all things, to explain a promise to come. At this time in my life, I had just come through some very difficult times that had left some apparent loose ends and questions about what was to come. During this season, I was diligently pursuing God's purposes, as well as the answers to the many questions at hand. He then spoke to me a promise that I will never forget. He not only showed what was to come, but ran this promise parallel with Habakkuk 2:3, "For still the vision awaits its appointed time; it hastens to the end—it will not lie. If it seems slow, wait for it; it will surely come."

Right about the time God spoke to me about how this promise would come but the completion would tarry, I came home one day to find a turtle just sitting on my doorstep. I couldn't believe it. It was as if someone had just placed it there. At the time, I didn't live anywhere near water and certainly not by creeks or streams. It was a typical developed neighborhood with streets, sidewalks, streetlights, and well-groomed yards. The only living thing that you would see passing by in this development besides a human on a bike was their pet on a leash as they walked nearby. This turtle on my doorstep was so out of the ordinary that I knew something was behind it. Not only was the location nowhere near the habitat of turtles or any other reptiles for that matter, but there was also the way it was just sitting at my doorstep, literally facing my door as if waiting for me to let him in. On top of all that, my house sat up on an elevation, leaving the concrete walkway on a somewhat steep angle for even getting up to my front door.

When I found out God was once more conveying a message through nature, I now had a new little friend. This turtle became my pet for the next season. This one was very easy to figure out. What, above all else, do turtles represent? They are *very slow.* This was exactly the pace at which this recently revealed promise would unfold. It was exactly as God had said in conjunction with Habakkuk 2:3. That is why this turtle was sent. It was a sign in nature—sent by God to my very doorstep of destiny—that the promise would come. It was also a wonder displaying how long this promise would actually take to fulfill. In other words, it was God saying, "Although it will be slow in coming, as this turtle represents, it will not lie. Although it may tarry, as it was brought to your very doorstep, I assure you it will come to pass." Boy, did I ever need that. Little did I know that this promise would take eight years to unfold. This new part of the family, Franklin was his name, became a daily reminder of the tarried promise to come.

God has used so many wonders through nature displays over the years—a dove, a snake, even a cardinal to name a few—that this realm can also become commonplace in the life of following Him. All that being said, God has and always will use nature as one of the main outlets of His voice to you and I. We must merely be attentive to hearing and knowing His voice by whichever means it comes.

Prayer

God, I thank You that You speak through nature and the very creation which You direct. Let these wonders of nature begin to break out in our lives, I pray, that we might walk in sync with You.

Chapter 4

ATMOSPHERIC WONDERS

ATMOSPHERIC WONDERS ARE INCREDIBLE DISPLAYS OF GOD'S VOICE through supernatural shifts in the atmosphere as a sign. I have seen the Lord do this time and time again with great accuracy and purpose. To bring our attention to His voice and plan, He causes the atmosphere itself to take on great shifts, even historic at times. Joel 2 states very clearly that in the latter days God will perform wonders in the heavens and signs in the earth (see Joel 2:30-31). Daniel 6:27 also says, "He works signs and wonders in heaven and on earth." These wonders in the heavens are exactly what I am referring to as atmospheric wonders. God will cause comets to come forth in certain seasons to convey His thoughts. He will even speak through whirlwinds, as mentioned in Psalms 77:18, "The crash of your thunder was in the whirlwind." We also see in Job 38:1 that God spoke to Job directly from out of a whirlwind. This would also happen to a well-known prophet of old, whom many of you have probably heard of, named William Branham. Since he was a young boy, there would appear an atmospheric wonder nearby in the form of a whirlwind, and God's angelic messenger would speak directly to him from that sign.

You will discover moving forward that God will not only speak parabolically through the wonder, but in many cases He will communicate literally from the platform of that very sign. Another good example of this—although I would not necessarily categorize it as an *atmospheric* wonder—was when God spoke to Moses out of the burning bush. As if the burning bush was not already a profound wonder to start with, God then proceeded to speak out of it to His chosen deliverer of the children of God.

Biblical Accounts of Atmospheric Wonders

The rainbow with Noah was an atmospheric sign and wonder— God was confirming that He would never again flood the earth. God also performed another astonishing atmospheric wonder that has never happened before or since when He made the sun stand still at the voice and prayer of Joshua until His children would come out victorious in battle (see Josh. 10:1-14). We also see an astonishing wonder performed through the atmosphere when the plague of hail was released upon Pharaoh's officials who did not fear the Lord (see Exod. 9). God held back the rain as an atmospheric sign and wonder of judgment and His favor lifting from Israel (see Amos 4:7-8). Zechariah 9:14 states clearly that God moves "in the *whirlwinds* of the south." The three-year drought followed by an utter deluge was an atmospheric wonder orchestrated by God through the prayer of Elijah. Then, fire from heaven came down at the prayer of Elijah (see 1 Kings 18). That also was an atmospheric sign.

Like the fire from the sky, I believe there will be many more atmospheric signs that are purely supernatural. Obviously, fire is not a natural manifestation that just appears out of the sky. But if you check Joel 2:30 it mentions very clearly that there will be signs in the heavens and wonders on the earth—blood, fire, and columns of smoke. Many logically believe that these appearances of blood, fire, and smoke will be natural results of war, famine, and bloodshed. But if that were true, then these manifestations that are to appear in the latter days would clearly not be *wonders*. They would be natural results, causes and effects with natural implications. That is why it is very important that we do not get our natural mind in the way of what Scripture makes very clear. It says what it says: "And I will show *wonders in the heavens* and on the earth, blood and fire and columns of smoke" (Joel 2:30).

With that being said, God will operate in both supernatural wonders in the atmosphere as well as *naturally* supernatural manifestations. Whirlwinds do appear. These would be natural atmospheric occurrences that God supernaturally orchestrates for His purpose and plan. Fire does not naturally appear in the atmosphere, although God will also use this type of wonder to get His message across to those who have ears to hear.

Atmospheric Wonder in Stars

God will also use stars to transmit His voice. A great biblical account of this was Jesus' birth. A star was sent by God that literally lead people to the precise geographical location of the newborn Son of God. "When they had heard the king, they departed; and, lo, the star, which they saw in the east, went before them, till it came and stood over where the young child was. When they saw the star, they rejoiced with exceeding great joy" (Matt. 2:9-10 KJV).

This still blows my mind every time I read it. I think too often we've been lulled to sleep, spiritually speaking, on many profound accounts of God's nature and voice. We see Christmas plays year after year, or hear cute Bible stories put into seasonal twists. All along, the God of wonders has been moving and speaking through astonishing means, and to this day He remains the same. I'm afraid, at times, just as we lack spiritual intuitiveness in these biblical events and the nature of His voice, that we, the body of Christ at large, are likewise missing the majority of what God is saying and trying to fulfill generation after generation.

One thing is certain. God is always speaking and will always continue to speak because of His deep sincerity of love and compassion toward humankind. He let His very own Son be killed for you and me, my friend. The Son of God lay down His life that we may know Him, the Holy Spirit, and the heavenly Father as one. To this day, Jesus has holes in each hand and holes in each foot—living proof of the highest paid price ever recorded in all of history. Why, you ask? That He might be in loving relationship with you and me.

You might say, "Well, what does this have to do with atmospheric wonders?" Everything! This whole thing is about loving relationship, intimate knowledge, and communicating one on one with the God of one true love. My point in all of this is that, with utmost priority and significance, we must learn how to hear the voice of our Maker, growing deeper in knowing and reflecting His greatness. One of the main ways He happens to communicate, especially in the last days, is through the performance of signs and wonders. We cannot continue falling short in this area. Of course we will make mistakes. Of course we will miss the mark here and there. But that is why we have a God of compassion, mercy, and love. Keep moving forward in this journey of intimately knowing the God of one true love. There is no greater goal. There is no higher prize. If you haven't until this day, I adjure you, my friend, to make Him, His voice, His presence and plan the number-one priority in all of your life.

Can you imagine God using a literal star in the atmosphere to not only appear before your very eyes, but to then move and guide you with utmost sovereignty and precision for His will and direction? This is exactly what He did in the account of the newborn Son of God. Why didn't He just come right out and tell the wise men where the Savior of the world would be born? Because once again, my friend, this is just who God is and how God chooses to speak. He uses signs and wonders as the very tablet upon which He inscribes for humankind the messages of eternity. It just comes down to—who will hear and who will perceive? I would highly advise you to learn how to read the language of wonders. Wisdom will begin leading you to discern the voice of the sign. He is continually speaking through wonders—abroad and worldwide, generation to generation—for the sake of His will.

Gateway to the United States

I remember a very profound atmospheric wonder that God performed several years back in the state of Virginia. I will never forget this trip, which brought about many prolific events. It happened that on the day of my arrival for several days of ministry in the state of Virginia, I was simultaneously completing a 40-day fast. The Lord had shown me months prior in a vision the exact days that He wanted me to go on this fast, set apart for Him and kingdom purposes. At that time, I had no idea this fast would lead me right up to my arrival in the state of Virginia, which I later figured out was nothing short of God-ordained.

You see, I have a very strong calling and divine assignment to the United States of America. And the state of Virginia is the actual doorway, if you will, to the US. Virginia is where everything started. Virginia is the gateway and birthing point of North America. I later found out that God was going to use me in a profound way during my first ministry visit to this national landmark. He would also confirm the nationwide call that He had been giving me all along.

I want to point out that there are many nations across the world that God has called our ministry to have great impact in. I have been to many regions already and continue to go. I love all the various cultures, people groups, and languages. There are actually very few national people groups worldwide that we have not invested into. This is why Bridal Glory International is without a doubt an international ministry. We want to see every tribe, every tongue, and every nation come to know the Lord Jesus Christ. But in this case, God went out of His way to confirm with wonders the nationwide call I was born to.

Several weeks prior to this time of ministry in Virginia, I was shown a vision in parallel with the days of Noah, when the springs of water burst up from the deep: "In the six hundredth year of Noah's life, in the second month, on the seventeenth day of the month, on that day all the fountains of the great deep burst forth, and the windows of the heavens were opened" (Gen. 7:11). This was obviously the beginning of the flood due to worldwide sin. In my vision, there were underwater aquifers bursting up through the ground's surface, like in the days of Noah. Furthermore, there was revelation of both state and nationwide sin in need of repentance.

Now this is where God gets ultra-specific if you pay attention to how and when He speaks. In breaking down the revelation from this vision, as I always tend to do, I noticed one profound detail of great interest and confirmation—the month and day upon which the flood began. If you read closely in Genesis 7:11, you will find that the waters burst forth from underground on the second month and seventeenth day. To my surprise, the day of my arrival in Virginia would fall out precisely upon the second month and seventeenth day, just as mentioned in Scripture. Another astonishing factor that played into this event was that this day would be the final day of the 40-day fast that I was on. Needless to say, God was certainly up to something and I was thrilled to be a part of it.

Intricacy of Knowing Him

It never ceases to amaze me how intricate God is with details. He will tie in exact timelines, dates, and seasons like a masterful work of art or the most complicated puzzle you have ever seen. Just think about it for a minute. You are dealing with the God of all creation, planets, animals, and the sea. He created every insect, down to the vast assortment of beautifully color-marbled butterflies. He created the ocean, the tides, and all that reside within. He created the ozone, the earth, humankind for all to see, the birds of the air, the beasts of the land, and all for you and me. If all of creation is merely what came out of who He is and what He likes to do, just imagine the depth of communication and articulation He can convey in loving relationship with humankind. Oh, that we might have listening ears to hear what He would say. God, I pray that I would be the recipient of all things in loving and knowing You. Let us know You more each day, building upon Your voice, I pray, this day and all the years to come, the place of Your presence our to and from.

These are the reasons why I stress the necessity of stewarding the voice of God. When you really begin to dig in to the nature of how He speaks, for what reason, why, and when, you will discover endless mysteries full of life, knowledge, wisdom, and power like you've never known before. He is in a league of His own, my friend, as He should be—He's God alone. I think far too often we minimize the capabilities and the possibilities through which He can communicate, only retaining a fraction of what He is really trying to say.

Necessity of Knowing Him

Let's move on toward the mark of the high prize in knowing Him. Let's no longer put off the life of invested love divine. After all, this whole thing is about Him. This whole thing is about knowing Him. This whole thing is about becoming just like Him. You're not going to get to heaven one day and be amazed at how great your earthly skill set or career played out, turning into some astounding eternal investment of ongoing interest. None of that will cross over. None of that will pass through. There will be many multi-millionaires baffled at how little they've invested into the kingdom of God. While storing up profound riches down here, to their amazement they will have zero-balance accounts in heaven. There will be people of great fame in the earth with no heavenly recognition whatsoever. Do not let the spirit of the age deter you, my friend. This whole thing is about Jesus. This whole thing is about loving Him. This whole thing is about obeying Him and making Him known.

Fasting: Not Optional

I got to Virginia a couple of belt loops lighter, if you know what I mean. Obviously, extended fasts will trim a few pounds off you, but at the same time they spiritually benefit you so much more. There are certain aspects of the kingdom that I personally believe one will never see come to fruition within their very own life apart from prayer and fasting. Fasting is an intricate part of God's purpose and plan, and an imperative necessity when walking out the life of Christ in you, the hope of glory.

Many people nowadays feel there is no more need to fast and pray, especially people carrying around this ever so rampant hyper-grace message. I assure you, my friend, the Bible is filled with spiritual hall-of-famers who fasted, like Moses, Elijah, David,

Daniel, Peter, Paul, not to mention Jesus, who continually fasted on multiple occasions. Paul even referred to being "in fastings often" (2 Cor. 11:27 KJV). Do not be fooled by this shallow message of the non-fasted life. There is even an account where the disciples tried to cast out a demon while carrying doubt and unbelief, and Jesus says, "This kind can come out by nothing but prayer and fasting" (Mark 9:29 NKJV). Don't be another plastic Christian, my friend, as the number is increasing in this day and age. Follow the heroes of the faith in the prayer and fasted life and watch heaven work alongside you like never before.

Supernatural Repentance

So I got to Virginia and had two days to minister in the Blacksburg area before leaving. Apart from seeing several other issues of ongoing sin that the Lord wanted me to address, I shared the vision of the underground waterways related to the need for repentance within that region and state, the gateway to our nation. I later found out that the land upon which I was ministering had two major underground waterways that everybody knew about. This obviously raised the confirmation level up a few more notches, as you can imagine.

To my amazement, even though this was one of the main Christian groups in that region, we had an altar call. People began to come up, repenting of just about everything under the sun. Homosexuality, drunkenness, pornography, and the list goes on and on. What was really fascinating about this night was that, as the spirit of repentance came, the grace and vulnerability of God came too. It was such an amazing thing to see. Often people feel quite hindered and embarrassed to come forth and repent of sinful decisions and ways of life, but there came such an openness and public repentance like I have never seen before or since. People began to initiate their own repentance, as if to get it off their chest. It was as if a fatherly love from heaven enabled this openness and freedom to come forth as people were being made whole and clean.

Historical Shift in the Atmosphere

Immediately following ministry that weekend in Blacksburg came an atmospheric wonder of historic proportions. The Saturday in Virginia before the Sunday of departure was a beautiful sun-shining day of around 80 degrees. There were people riding bikes, playing volleyball with their shirts off, and throwing the Frisbee while drinking smoothies—in February. It was an amazing day, needless to say, and it actually had not snowed that whole winter season up until this point. Would you believe that the day following, the Sunday I flew out, a monumental, historic snow swept through the region? The region got eight inches of snow, baffling the locals, weather forecasters, and scientists alike. Prior to this historic atmospheric shift, there was popular belief that snow could not stick to the ground after temperatures as warm as the day before. Renewing the minds of the unbelievers if you will, they certainly now knew that it was quite possible. The thickest snowfall was actually in Blacksburg itself, where we were ministering, and then the inches of snow began to diminish out from that point. An atmospheric shift of this magnitude had not happened in over 80 years of recorded history. This incident took over news and newspaper headlines alike, as you can imagine. It brought about immediate regional change. One day people were riding bikes and playing beach volleyball; the next day people were sledding down hills, building snowmen, and throwing snowballs.

White as Snow

Snow in Scripture refers to purity. White is the color of holiness, without spot or blemish. When God sends an atmospheric sign of snow to a region, following a message of repentance foreseen by vision and parallel with Scripture, it is something to behold. Job 38:22 says, "Have you entered the storehouses of the snow?" This was an atmospheric wonder performed by God, backing up the message of repentance and holiness needed in this region. It was also a sign of holiness blanketing and sweeping through. We must pay attention to these types of activities; they are God's confirming signs and communications through atmospheric wonders. When you see weather patterns shift like they haven't in almost a century, you might want to pay attention to it. Even if it didn't directly tie in to what God had you doing in the region, it is still very important to keep up with what God is doing and saying, and why. I often will be shown what God is doing all over the world in different regions directly tied in to atmospheric wonders. It doesn't matter if God used me to initiate the sign or not. It's just about His will being done in the earth and knowing Him and why He does what He does.

Supernatural Ray of Light Caught on Camera

In closing the ministry visit to Virginia, there was a profound occurrence involving a photograph I want to point out. This will also give you a chance to see the snow that blanketed the region, as this was the whole point behind taking the photograph in the first place.

Six months before visiting Virginia, the Lord took me into a vision at 12:01 p.m. one day, just past noon. Wide awake, I literally went into this vision of the Lord in the heavens, as a portal opened from above. Just as fast as the Lord pulled open this portal to heaven, a beam of the light of His glory came down that was so white and bright that it was without a doubt blinding for the naked eye to see. Upon seeing this light, the vision ended, thank the good Lord above—this was far too bright for anyone to behold for any length of time. I journaled this vision, of course, and later found out that the Lord was speaking to me in parallel with the apostle Paul. There was an apostolic/prophetic call upon my life similar to Paul's. Also, Paul was commissioned to a specific people group when he was blinded by the light of God's glory on the road to Damascus. This again will show you how specific God is in speaking to you, whether it be by vision, dream, sign, or wonder.

As I mentioned earlier, I was taken into that vision at 12:01 p.m. Well, at the end of the book of Acts, as Paul was giving his testimony to King Agrippa, he stated, "About noon, King Agrippa, as I was on the road, I saw a light from heaven, brighter than the sun, blazing around me and my companions" (Acts 26:13 NIV). This was the reason why I very well could have been in the vision right at 12 noon, because I checked the time as I was coming out of the vision, as I have learned to do. The vision at noon was a direct parallel with Paul's heavenly blinding light and his commissioning encounter happening at noon. So, lo and behold, six months later I was in Virginia, right in the middle of this atmospheric wonder experience following the message from the Lord. I all of a sudden felt the urge to get a photograph taken as a memory of what God did, and that very same beam of God's glory showed up in the photograph right over my right shoulder. (See fig. J in Appendix.)

I thought, *Why on earth did You wait this long for this light, which I saw months and months ago, to be caught on camera?* The Lord showed me that He was specifically waiting until I stepped foot into that region, because Virginia, once again, represents the birth of the US. He wanted to make a statement like that which he did to Paul. My call is similar in prophetic and apostolic nature, as well as to what people group I would be sent.

Winds of Change

Another profound atmospheric wonder that God worked through was not too long ago in the beautiful state of Montana. I was there ministering for about twelve days straight in three different regions. We were leaving one city after several days of ministry and stopping for only two nights of ministry in another before moving on to the final destination. One of our stops was a major university campus in the town we were passing through. The day before ministering on campus, some friends and I decided to take a leisurely hike up a mountain directly across from the university. The view was astonishing, with a complete oversight of the campus, surrounding landscape, nearby river, and bridge.

The next morning, I was in prayer concerning the Lord's heart for that campus and region, as we would be ministering to them that evening. I went into a vision of Jesus sitting up on the side of the mountain we had hiked the day before. He was overlooking the campus. He had a fan in His right hand and was holding it out over the campus. I came out of the vision and journaled it. The Lord later showed me that what I was seeing was the exact same thing mentioned in Matthew 3:12, "His winnowing fan is in His hand, and He will thoroughly clean out His threshing floor" (NKJV). This Scripture refers to cleansing and purging that which is not from Him—clearing out darkness and sin.

A winnowing fan is a broad, flat basket which farmers put grain into. They then toss the grain into the air, and the inedible husks break off and are carried away by the wind, leaving only the grain itself. This Scripture describes darkness being removed with an analogy of a winnowing fan working with the wind to purge that which will soon be discarded.

Only hours after this vision, that same afternoon a vicious windstorm swept through the region. Most of the impact was the university campus. After ministry that evening, people on campus were all talking about the crazy windstorm that came out of nowhere. Once again, this paranormal atmospheric shift made newspaper headlines. Trees were uprooted, power lines were down, cars were destroyed.

The next day following this abnormal windstorm on the college campus, the head football coach and the athletic director were fired amidst a collection of rape and sexual assault charges involving the university's football team members. This also made local newspaper headlines, as you can imagine. The head football coach went from consecutive winning seasons and actually being voted as coach of the year within this university's conference to an immediate dismissal, along with the athletic director, to everyone's surprise.

The Lord purged these sin issues the day immediately following this ever-so-peculiar windstorm on campus. To this day, the timing has not been fully explained—the conference's coach of the year and the athletic director were suddenly fired the day following this bizarre windstorm. If you do not have ears to hear what the Spirit is saying, these types of incidents will go right over your head. Actually, they go on all the time with the very voice of God Almighty right in the middle of them. Even if the occasion brings about back-to-back newspaper headlines, most people will completely miss what is really going on in and through each event. I was thankfully given foresight of what was to come, which was the major key to knowledge and understanding concerning the atmospheric sign. At the same time, however, it is very easy to miss what God is saying and doing if you do not steward His voice and mysteries alike.

Do Not Despise Seasons of Preparation

One very profound atmospheric wonder is a very dear memory to me. Several years before this atmospheric sign took place, I was in prayer one day in my office. At this time in my life, I had been involved in little to no ministry concerning the purpose and destiny of God upon my life. Although my greatest passion in life was to be used by God—whatever that may look like—this season found me in more of a waiting period, which I have since come to enjoy. These preparation seasons are some of the greatest times that I can remember.

In a season of waiting, you have countless hours to just be with Him, to be consumed in His presence, and to bask in His voice. There is nothing quite like being with Him in deep intimacy with no agenda or plan—just 100 percent in relationship and knowing His love. It's just you and Him, one on one, knowing His thoughts, His heart, and His concerns. We should obviously maintain a loving relationship day in and day out, but there is something special about spending weeks and months on end loving and being loved for hours upon hours a day. It is unmatchable in life's journey of knowing Him. I love how David describes this: "One thing have I asked of Lord, that will I seek after: that I may dwell in the house of Lord all the days of my life, to gaze upon the beauty of Lord and to inquire in his temple" (Ps. 27:4). I also love how Mark writes: "And he appointed twelve...*that they might be with him* and he might send them out to preach" (Mark 3:14).

You will notice in God's design for kingdom commissioning, the *being with Him* part will always precede the *going*. You can never be sent forth from a place you've not been. You can never represent something or someone you do not know. You can never have impact for a King you've not known. All that being said, my friend, *never* neglect the seasons of preparation—knowing and loving Him.

The Vision of Being Sent

In the office that day while in prayer, I was taken into an astounding vision. I was in an open land, and I could see two massive tornados far off in the distance. They were enormous, making nearby power lines and trees look like Monopoly game pieces. These two tornados were not only spinning with great force and wind power, they were strategically coming right at me. Still about several football fields away from where I was standing, the tornados both paused for a moment, spinning in place.

One marvelous thing about this vision was that the interpretation came with it. As I saw things take place, I immediately knew in my spirit what each element represented. This is often not the case in visions and dreams. You will usually have to come out of the vision or dream and then hold it before the Lord in prayer and begin to interpret it, sometimes for hours and days. Needless to say, I was very thankful for this self-interpreted vision, as I have had far fewer of them than visions that do need interpretation. When this happens, it is as if the Spirit of wisdom and understanding is intertwined into the vision or dream itself. As these tornados paused for a moment, I immediately knew that this was how far out from hitting me they were in my life. I also knew that the massive tornado on the left represented revelation and the matching tornado on the right represented power.

The vision continued, and the tornados began on their path toward me again. As they got closer and closer I could see a glowing being between them, as if this angelic being was actually carrying them in each hand. Arriving before me in the vision, this angel slammed these two tornados right into me. It reminded me of people clanging cymbals together. That is exactly how this glowing angelic being sandwiched me between these two huge tornados.

I then left my body in the vision to see what would unfold. I could now see everything from a bird's-eye view. Looking down, I was being spun and thrown around like a rag doll in what was now one tornadic unit of revelation and power. To my utter amazement, I was then spit or thrust out from this whirlwind and launched from my homeland of Louisiana up to Pennsylvania of all places. I hit Pennsylvania like a pinball would hit an obstruction in a pinball machine, and then was thrust all over the nation and then the world. The vision ended. You can imagine, although the interpretation did come with this vision, I was still thinking, *What was that all about?*

Ever since that vision, I not only knew that a big part of my calling would be being sent forth from a place of revelation and power, but it would somehow begin and go through the state of Pennsylvania. At that time in my life, this seemed virtually impossible. I knew absolutely no one from Pennsylvania and had no connections whatsoever. I honestly wasn't even sure where Pennsylvania was. Thankfully, the vision came with all of those details, or I would have had to search the Internet to find out what state that actually was up there in the northeast.

The Tornados Finally Arrive

Years and years went by following this commissioning vision—seven to be exact. Year after year I anticipated the arrival of these great forces of revelation and power that were going to somehow employ me through the great state of Pennsylvania. I had journaled this foreseen event and even told dear friends. I didn't know how on God's green earth this imperative thrusting point would come to pass, but someway and somehow the Lord would first take me directly to the state of Pennsylvania and then to the nations of the world.

Lo and behold, a door opened up for me to go minister in Harrisburg, Pennsylvania. As you can imagine, I did not require much prayer to see if this was the will of the Lord or not. At this point in my life, I had already been ministering and traveling a bit here and there, but in the back of my head I always knew that things would not officially begin until heaven fulfilled this commissioning through the great northeast. The door that opened up to minister was at Randy Clark's Global Awakening base in Harrisburg, Pennsylvania called the School of the Supernatural. A friend and I would be preaching, teaching, and prophesying over first- and second-year students. By the way, if you are considering a Bible college to attend, I would certainly consider this one. There is such a rich presence of God in this place, ever-present upon the students, producing a profound hunger and passion. They join a biblical foundation with the Spirit's power and demonstration. I would highly recommend this school for anyone considering ministry.

Prior to this trip to Pennsylvania, I had experienced several angelic encounters on paramount levels, clearly imparting these forces of revelation and power. These fulfilled the part of the vision where the glowing angelic being slammed the tornados of revelation and power into me. But now, here came the actual thrusting point that would send me up to Pennsylvania. The day of my departure came, and I was on the treadmill that morning getting a little exercise before heading to the airport to catch my flight. I remember missing a call from a family member—quite an unusual call, at that time of the day. On the way home from the gym, I checked my voicemail. This family member was concerned, as there were tornado outbreaks surrounding the region. They knew I would be flying out that day and were worried that the flights would not be free to depart—and they worried for my safety if they did.

I got home to finish packing for my trip and turned on the weather report. To my amazement, in all of the US there was only one strange weather pattern going on that day, which was catching everyone's eye. There was a precise weather band of tornado-producing winds starting from the southern tip of Louisiana—exactly where I would be flying out of—and swinging clear up to the state of Pennsylvania. It was the strangest thing you've ever seen. The weather across the whole continent of North America was just as calm and dormant as it could possibly be, and then all of a sudden you see this wild, tornado-producing wind force that formed a precise weather band starting in Louisiana and leading right up to Pennsylvania.

This was it! The vision was unfolding! After seven years of longing for this great geographic commissioning, it was finally here. On top of that, God went out of His way to kindly confirm what He had told me many years before with an atmospheric wonder.

Whirlwind Wonder

I would like to briefly share another exciting wonder that happened through a whirlwind. Again, God's voice is threaded all throughout wonders, whether to confirm something *to* you or even confirm a message *through* you. There are many ways that God operates and speaks through signs and wonders. The point is to learn how to hear His voice in the sign, so that we might work alongside Him for His kingdom and purpose, all while remaining caught up in loving communion with the Lover of our souls.

One night, I went into a profound dream where I was literally going through a massive whirlwind. As the whistling and swirling winds whipped all around me in this dream, I knew in my spirit that it somehow connected with William Branham. I checked my phone to see what time it was. There were two times on my phone, 4:05 and 1:38. I later realized that these two times were directly tied in to William Branham's two most favorite and quoted verses, Malachi 4:5 and Hebrews 13:8. This was the reason I saw these times within this whirlwind while understanding that it all somehow connected to William Branham. This was one of many parallels in which the Lord has compared my calling to his. It is very helpful when the Lord does this, as it brings great insight and understanding. He shows you why you are wired the way you are and why you hear His voice the way you do. He'll use this for kingdom purposes, your destiny, and life in general.

Many do not know this, but William Branham was followed by a whirlwind on numerous occasions as a young boy and even into adulthood. There was even an occasion where the voice of an angel sent from God came out of the whirlwind and spoke to him, telling him to remain pure as a little boy, because he would have a great work to do for the kingdom when he grew up. Later in life, following another one of these whirlwind appearances, that very same angel appeared to commission him. He began to reveal many things concerning William Branham's call: "As John the Baptist was the forerunner of the first coming of the Lord, you (William Branham) will be the forerunner of the second coming of the Lord."

Not only did John the Baptist come in the Spirit of Elijah, as Scripture clearly states, but Elijah himself was also directly tied in to whirlwinds. "And as they still went on and talked, behold, chariots of fire and horses of fire separated the two of them. And Elijah went up by a whirlwind into heaven" (2 Kings 2:11). Elijah was caught up in a whirlwind when the chariot of fire came down to separate Elisha from Elijah. Many think that Elijah went up in the chariot; you will even see this depicted in modern-day art, but this is not what Scripture says. The Bible says the chariot came and separated Elisha from Elijah, and then Elijah was taken up in a whirlwind. The chariot of fire merely separated them before Elijah was caught up in the whirlwind.

Whirlwinds as atmospheric wonders, I believe, were a common feature of the life and ministry of Elijah. This is another key focal point to watch with God. When He chooses a certain wonder to perform in speaking to you, there is also a message in that sign. God was always drawing parallels between my life and William Branham, and I began to wonder, *Why on earth did God continually show up in the specific wonder of a whirlwind while speaking to him?* Then one day the light bulb went off. It was because he was commissioned in the same manner of John the Baptist, *in the Spirit of Elijah*, as the angel said. And who was the general of God most directly tied to whirlwinds? Elijah! Now it all made sense. You will notice this with God as you pay more and more attention. He will speak through repetitive threads of wondrous signs to communicate His intent and purpose behind your calling and reason for being. This dream contained scriptural parallels filtered through my phone—I would like to point out that phones in dreams and visions typically speak of your calling or destiny.

Shortly following the dream came the whirlwind itself. I had already figured out the meaning of 4:05 and 1:38—the two times on my phone were connected with William Branham's life verses, Malachi 4:5 and Hebrews 13:8. I was also aware that the whirlwind in the dream was connected to the manifested wonder that followed his life. Several days after the dream, following this breakdown of exuberant revelation, I was driving down a major highway when, to my surprise, there it was! A whirlwind hovering over the road! I was astounded at how symmetrically centered it remained over the two-lane highway I was traveling upon. I was immediately brought back to the dream. In my mind I knew, *This is it!* I knew that this was a confirming wonder of the foretold dream. With great excitement, as if heading to the finish line in a race, I swerved to the center of both lanes. I wanted to make sure and drive straight through the center of this profound manifestation and wondrous sign.

Thank God that He knows just what is safe and what is not. Although this whirlwind was just large enough to hover over the two lanes of highway and fully envelope my automobile, it was safe enough that I found myself in one piece on the other side. The whirling winds and leaves then began to dissipate. I backtracked to the exact place this whirlwind manifested on the highway, in order to confirm the dream. Would you believe it? It was precisely on the city boundary line—the city to which the Lord had called me as my base, the area I was to impact. The whirlwind manifested on the highway right at the boundary of the Lord-appointed city.

The Deluge of the Dominican Republic

I will share one last atmospheric wonder that was absolutely fascinating, which God performed in the beautiful nation of the Dominican Republic. Some dear friends and I were in Santo Domingo for one whole week, preaching the gospel followed by healings, miracles, signs, and wonders. We had an amazing time preaching and teaching the gospel while many people were touched and transformed by the power of God. The last Sunday morning we were ministering in the Dominican Republic before flying out early the following day, I was preaching on my favorite subject of all—intimacy with Jesus. There is no higher call. There is no higher purpose. Intimately knowing and walking with the Lord Jesus Christ is the whole reason for living, as far as I am concerned. Everything else follows far behind that. If you ever get sidetracked from the loving relationship of knowing Him, you have certainly missed the mark and need to adamantly return.

On the way to church that morning, it was a bright and sun-shiny day. There was not a cloud in the sky, and it was very hot, I might add. I preached on loving Jesus and maintaining intimacy like never before. We laid hands on the sick, and many were healed, set free, and touched mightily by the power of God. I concluded the meeting and went to sit down. The moment my backside hit the chair, this absolute deluge from heaven come down. It went from the most beautiful day of luminous sun rays to an instant downpour of rain like you have never seen. The climatic shift and weather transformation immediately followed the exact time the meeting closed. We instantly knew that God was confirming the message by way of an atmospheric sign.

Later that evening, we found out from a regional pastor that Santo Domingo had been in a six-month drought. We began to thank God for the downpour of rain that came to their city that day. It was quite profound. I believe it was not only a confirmation of God's kiss upon the message and our presence in that region, but also His divine favor and blessing that was coming to this region as they began to steward the highest call of intimacy with Him.

Prayer

God, I thank You that the atmosphere around us was created by You, through You, and for You to relate and sustain the fruition of Your will. I pray that You would begin to release and increase Your mighty atmospheric signs and wonders in these last days like never before. Let Your world break into ours, I pray, while we discern and coincide with Your voice and desired plan. Be glorified, oh God, in wonders of Your display.

Chapter 5

WONDERS IN THE EARTH

IN THIS CHAPTER I WILL BE DISCUSSING GOD'S PERFORMANCE AND display of signs and wonders within the earth. There are two foundational verses here—"I will show wonders in the heavens and *on the earth*" (Joel 2:30), and, "He works signs and wonders in heaven and on earth" (Dan. 6:27). While the previous chapter was dealing strictly with atmospheric wonders—or, as the Bible calls them, "wonders in the heavens"—this chapter will be going over many specific ways that God performs "wonders in the earth."

Biblical Accounts of Wonders in the Earth

Where do you begin when it comes to God's display of wonders in the earth? There are so many throughout all of Scripture that you could pretty much devote a whole book to their exclusive workings alone. David could not have said it any better: "Many, O Lord my God, are Your wonderful works which You have done" (Ps. 40:5 NKJV). You can look from the Old Testament all the way through the New and one common thread you are certain to find is the glorious wonders of God being displayed throughout the earth from generation to generation.

Wonders of Moses

The wonders in the earth performed by God through Moses were obviously paramount in all of history. Among many others, you have the staff turning into a snake, the leprous transformation of his hand, display of wondrous plagues, turning water into blood, parting the Red Sea, striking the rock that produced water, his face shining with light, and the Israelites' clothes/shoes never wearing out after 40 years in the wilderness. The list just keeps on going.

Fleece of Gideon

There was also the wonder God performed when Gideon needed confirmation of his calling.

> Then Gideon said to God, "If you will save Israel by my hand, as you have said, behold, I am laying a fleece of wool on the threshing floor. If there is dew on the fleece alone, and it is dry on all the ground, then I shall know that you will save Israel by my hand, as you have said." And it was so. When he rose early next morning and squeezed the fleece, he wrung enough dew from the fleece to fill a bowl with water. Then Gideon said to God, "Let not your anger burn against me; let me speak just once more. Please let me test just once more with the fleece. Please let it be dry on the fleece only, and on all the ground let there be dew." And God did so that night; and it was dry on the fleece only, and on all the ground there was dew (Judges 6:36-40).

I love this sign and wonder that God performed, bringing certainty and confirmation to that which Gideon had already been told. One thing about God is that He is so loving, compassionate, slow to anger, and full of mercy that He will gladly confirm what He has told you time and time again if that is what it takes for you to walk out the highest destiny of what He has called you to do. This is entirely different from the spirit of the Pharisees and Sadducees, who had to have a sign to even believe in the first place. Gideon had full faith, he just wanted reassurance and further confirmation that he was hearing correctly and doing the right thing. This was a very risky task and costly endeavor which he was about to embark upon.

God always looks at the heart. If you have a willing heart and a desire to obey, He will gladly go out of His way to reiterate what He has told you by way of sign and wonder. I have seen Him do this over and over again in my own life, especially when it came down to something of great significance and costly measure. But if you want to come to God with this Pharisaical spirit of "prove it" or "if You don't perform a sign I won't believe it," you can forget about it. You will certainly be setting yourself up for a life free of signs and wonders. You believe; then you see.

Jonah and the Tree

I absolutely love this wonder in the earth that God performed. The God of all creation, the universe, and beyond went out of His way to cause one simple tree to supernaturally grow in a single day in order to bring shade to one prophet in all the earth—Jonah. Let's look at the account: "Now the Lord God appointed a plant and made it come up over Jonah, that it might be a shade over his head, to save him from his discomfort. So Jonah was exceedingly glad because of the plant" (Jonah 4:6).

Now we know the whole story—how Jonah got mad and a bit out of order at the end—but that's another story. I can hardly blame him, and until I walk in his shoes I have no room whatsoever to say I would have handled it any better. One thing we can do with the story, though, is learn from it. And there's one thing for sure that I love about this account—God's amazing wonder in the earth for one man in all of creation, Jonah. What an amazing God. He caused a tree to grow over the head of Jonah as shade, saving him from discomfort. Amazingly, later in Scripture He tied the wonder of the tree in to the concluding lesson which Jonah learned.

Wonders, Wonders, Wonders

There were so many more accounts of earthly wonders that God performed throughout Scripture again and again and again. Shadrach, Meshach, and Abednego did not burn up in the fiery furnace, and a fourth Guest made an appearance (see Dan. 3:8-30). Elisha made the axe head float (see 2 Kings 6:6). Jesus cursed the fig tree to its death; He also multiplied food (see Matt. 21:18-22; 14:13-21). Paul cast blindness upon a magician, resulting in the conversion of the proconsul (see Acts 13:8-12). Paul and Silas were freed from jail by an earthquake (see Acts 16:16-24). The wonders God did and continues to do, generation after generation, are completely innumerable in quantity while all rooted in the depth of His love. Each and every sign and wonder that God does is with great purpose and strategic intent. As I begin to go into personal experiences with wonders in the earth, you will see further into how intricately God's love and voice is intertwined within each and every one.

God's Shaking Wonder

Not too long ago, I was preaching down in the beautiful nation of Colombia. Some dear friends and I were scheduled to be preaching there all week, around two to three times a day. We were teaching Bible school classes in the daytime and preaching revival healing services at night. A profound wonder in the earth was birthed on the very first night.

In the hotel room about midday, I lay down for a brief power nap before getting ready for the service that night. I was lying on my stomach and just began to doze off when an angel came up from behind me. My spiritual eyes were opened, enabling me to see this messenger. You see, when your spiritual eyes are opened to see into the eternal realm, you are not limited to mere peripheral vision, as is the case with natural eyesight. Spiritual eyesight, or seeing in the spirit, has no limits. You can see a panoramic view of 360 degrees. You can see directly behind you, over you, through physical matter, and even far-off distances that could never be attained through the natural human eye.

This is what happened in this case; I was enlightened to see this heavenly messenger come up directly behind me. He walked up and simply said, "I heard a judgment coming, and it really changed the dirt." I immediately knew that God was sending a judgment wake-up call to the nation of Colombia through an earthquake. I've seen the angelic realm facilitate many judgments by the voice and will of God; I knew that if it was going to "really change the dirt," this was certainly none other than a powerful earthquake. I journaled the words of the heavenly messenger in the notes section of my phone. I told no one about what I had just heard and continued the day.

On our way to service that night, I was thinking, *Oh, great! The first night and I have to release a word of judgment and God's loving correction. I'm sure this is going to go over real well.* (Sarcasm.) You see, my friend, it is one thing to be the mouthpiece when times are good and you have messages of God's promises and goodness coming to each and every one. But it is a whole different thing when you have to be the middle man for God's corrective order and righteous alignment in the earth. You can become very unpopular real quick to the eyes of man. That's why I can so relate to Jonah and how badly he did not want to release that word of judgment to Nineveh. For one thing, he knew how unfavorable this was in the eyes of man. And if you read closely, he knew that God would relent and withhold His judgment, thereby making Jonah look like a false prophet. However you look at it, my friend, this whole thing comes down to obedience. And I'm pretty sure the last time I checked the Bible says, "If I were still trying to please man, I would not be a servant of Christ" (Gal. 1:10). Another prevalent verse in this matter would be, "And do not fear those who kill the body but cannot kill the soul. Rather fear him who can destroy both soul and body in hell" (Matt. 10:28).

Nevertheless, I released the word of this soon-coming shaking and judgment as a wake-up call to the national sin of Colombia. The Holy Spirit enabled me to humbly release the word amidst many other examples of judgment which I had also been foreshown and had also come to pass. The whole goal in a situation like this is to try and get the people to return to God. So we did just that. On top of my dear friend having a very powerful altar call for salvation, we also corporately prayed for the nation of Colombia. We prayed that the nation's heart would turn back toward her Maker. We prayed that God would have mercy upon the precious nation of Colombia that He dearly loves so much. Lo and behold, exactly three weeks following this message, the largest earthquake in over eight years hit the capital city of Colombia. And all glory be to God, to the best of my knowledge and according to the news reports, there were no deaths and minimal destruction. I believe with all of my heart that if we had not been sent into the nation of Colombia in that hour and released the word of correction leading to repentance, things would have certainly been catastrophic on a much larger scale.

You see, God is slow to anger and abounding in love. He never judges first, but allows time for our hearts to turn to Him. He is quick to forgive, overflowing with mercy, but at the same time seated upon a throne of righteousness and justice with our greatest benefit in mind. As you see through this particular wonder in the earth, a nation that God loves so dearly was saved and preserved. Although we were not able to stop the earthquake entirely, we certainly lightened the blow, which I believe could have been much worse.

As I mentioned earlier, in Acts 16 God liberates Paul from jail with an earthquake, whereas this earthquake was a warning. That is another thing you must pay attention to when hearing God's voice through wonders—the application. How does it apply? What angle of communication is God coming from? And what is the ultimate purpose? We must always remember that, as a loving Father, God will not only confirm, exhort, encourage, and direct but warn and correct in the same manner. The Bible says very clearly that He disciplines those He loves, and we must always be open to correction and loving alignment from our heavenly Father.

Open Door of God's Wonder

Like God's wonder of the confirming fleece displayed to Gideon, I had a very similar experience occur. A dear friend of mine in ministry was visiting one weekend while preaching in a nearby church. One afternoon, we were discussing various things about the will of God when a profound wonder of confirmation occurred.

One thing I would love to interject about this is how amazing it is when believers come together and begin to commune and discuss the things of the Lord. All of heaven is attentive when the Lord is the focal point of earthly discussion. We see this very clearly in Malachi 3:16, "Then those who feared the Lord spoke with one another. The Lord paid attention and heard them, and a book of remembrance was written before him of those who feared the Lord and esteemed his name." There is just something about esteeming and lifting up the name of Jesus that triggers the kingdom of heaven around you. The kingdom of God is like a fire, and the name and presence of the Lord is the match. The logs are set in place and the gasoline is already poured on—as Jesus said, the kingdom of God is always near, accessible, and at hand. As soon as you begin to mention the glorious name and presence of Jesus, the match has been struck and the fire has started. Then it's too late, my friend—heaven has broken in.

So there we were, my dear friend and I, discussing the Lord and His will. One of the main puzzle pieces to the fruition of this wonder is the fact that my friend had invited me to come be on a ministry television shoot with him that was scheduled for a couple of months out. As we casually continued in kingdom conversation, all of a sudden my front door opened up in broad daylight with no one standing there. We both looked at each other, astonished and taken aback. I immediately checked the time, as I have learned to do with God's wonders over the years, and it was 1:24 p.m. Lo and behold, this was the exact month and day on the Hebrew calendar of the trip for this television shoot. God will speak with the Hebrew calendar just as much as our Gregorian calendar. He sees Jews and Gentiles alike through the precious blood of Jesus, as we are grafted in. It is crucial that you keep this in mind as you move forward in hearing His voice. We should adjust to His viewpoint and overall method of communication, rather than expect Him to always work within our limited understanding.

So here we had it, a wonder of God "opening a door." He was confirming that I should be involved with this friend's opportunity two months down the road. He not only made sure that the wonder manifested at the exact hour and minute parallel to the calendar month and day when this event would take place, but also aligned the sign so that I was actually in conversation with the very person who would offer this "open door." I tell you, my friend, when God desires His will to be done in the earth, He will go to any lengths to make sure that very thing gets done just as He so desires. All we have to do is listen and obey.

Feather of Approval

As if the open door were not confirmation enough that I was to do this ministry television shoot with my dear friend, several weeks prior to leaving I went to grab some airline papers that I had received in the mail from off of my kitchen counter top when this little white feather manifested in midair right before me at 4:16 p.m. Again, I checked the time, my surroundings, and what I was doing that triggered this sign to manifest. And there it was! A dual confirming sign! Just as Gideon received two signs with the fleece confirming one thing God had spoken, this same breakdown was now happening. Looking into why the feather manifested in midair right when I went to grab those specific airline papers, I soon found out that this was the same airline (that I typically do not fly) that my friend would be flying me over with for that trip. We already had a sign confirming this trip by the month and day on the Hebrew calendar, but guess what month and day this event would take place on our calendar? You guessed it, 4/16—April 16. This was not only why the feather manifested at the very hour and minute of 4:16, but also why I was prompted to grab the papers of the airline which I would be traveling with upon this God-ordained event. You see, God is not only very specific in tying in His voice to signs and wonders, but will also, by the Holy Spirit, prompt you to do things that will cause the actual sign to manifest.

Apostolic Wonder

Another wonder that God performed in the earth, I will surely never forget. I had just come to an end of a 40-day fast and was attending a conference up in Coeur d'Alene, Idaho. The title of the conference was "It's Time: Releasing Apostolic Power." It was during a season of my life before I had been released into ministry on any notable level. Nevertheless, I had a strong inclination to attend this conference.

Months before the conference, I had been prophesied over by a nationally-known prophetess. This prophetess was praying over me when she suddenly stopped as though the light bulb went off and began to say, "Clark Kent, Clark Kent, Clark Kent!" I thought, *What?* And she said, "Clark Kent—Superman," as she began to prophecy about me being a spiritual parallel to Superman while carrying an outer demeanor of Clark Kent in humility and meekness.

It was a very encouraging word that I received, then went about my day not thinking too much about it. Well, God obviously thought a bit more about it. Superman parallels began to literally haunt me for the next year in just about every form or fashion. Everywhere I would go it was Superman this or Superman that. I even had a powerful prophetic dream that God took me into one night where I was literally flying around like Superman—and I woke up with my hair even fixed like Superman. I know! I was just as taken aback by it as anyone else would have been. Waking up from the dream, I passed by the mirror and saw that exact same curl of hair coming down my forehead, just like Superman. God is so funny sometimes in the wonders and extent He will go to in communicating His purposes and heart to humankind.

After all the revelatory parallels to Superman following the prophetic word that I had received, I changed my ringtone to the Superman song. Can't you hear it now? *Duh-duh-duuuuuuh, duh-duh-duh-duh-duuuuuuuh!* Of course, in public I would always keep my phone on vibrate; it would sound way too arrogant to people who didn't know the implication behind it. But at home I would keep it on ring as a reminder of what God had said. I always like doing this regarding the voice of God. Whatever He might speak, I like to always keep it before me in continual reverence to His voice.

Months later, I found myself at this conference, "It's Time: Releasing Apostolic Power." I had kept my phone on vibrate all day as I was flying from airport to airport and traveling to Coeur d'Alene. Arriving to my hotel later that day, I wound down for the night, expectant for the conference kicking off the following day. I went to sleep, forgetting to set my phone back to ring. Lo and behold, right at 6:14 a.m., my phone rang anyway. *Duh-duh-du-uuuuuh, duh-duh-duh-duh-duuuuuuuh!* I thought, *Who on earth is calling me this early, and how is my phone even ringing while set on vibrate?* I checked my phone. My caller ID read "unknown caller" and then the call ended. I checked the settings, and sure enough the phone was still set on vibrate—it was not supposed to be capable of ringing.

I was a bit startled. Who could that have been? And the call itself was impossible; only supernatural intervention could have made the phone ring while on vibrate. I went to use the restroom, and it got even crazier. Passing by the mirror I noticed a hand print on my chest. I did a double take, and sure enough there it was. A literal hand print, dead center on my chest where the Superman emblem would be. Now I was really freaked out. In a matter of minutes, I suddenly had a lot to deal with. *Who called, how'd they make it ring, and what is this handprint on my chest?*

Thank God I had already learned to *mark the time*. This whole supernatural relay kicked off at 6:14 a.m. when the phone call came in. I waited upon the Lord with this handprint on my chest that remained for a half hour to an hour. Thank Jesus for the Spirit of wisdom and revelation as the understanding began to unfold. The Lord showed me that this supernatural call was ignited at 6:14 a.m. in parallel with Judges 6:14 and the apostolic commissioning of Gideon. "And the Lord turned to him and said, 'Go in this might of yours and save Israel from the hand of Midian; *do not I send you*?'" (Judg. 6:14).

You see, this conference I was now attending had triggered the whole thing. It's title was "It's Time: Releasing Apostolic Power," and the definition of an apostle is "one who is sent." We see Gideon commissioned this way in Judges 6:14 when God says, "Do not I send you?" Gideon was sent out from his "Clark Kent" stage— needing God's angelic "mighty man of valor" approval—to enter his Superman status of heroic proportions. In my case, God was performing a sign along with this conference, the apostolic call of release, and the previous prophetic word, all of which tied in to the call of Gideon. The Lord "called in" (which pertains to the "call") as an unknown caller at 6:14 a.m. (in connection with Judges 6:14) and then tied the whole thing in with a handprint right in the center of my chest where the heroic emblem would be placed. He was basically saying, *Duh-duh-duuuuuuh, duh-duh-duh-duh-duuuuuuuh!* "Am I not sending you?" "It's Time: Releasing Apostolic Power" was now here, confirmed through the conference and prophetic word. I tell you, God is something else at times, isn't He? His wonders and voice are so intermingled with excitement, fun, mystery, and meaning all in one. You'll never walk with anyone on a journey quite like this. Enjoy Him, my friend, as He expresses His will through His word, wonders, presence, and voice.

The Vine of Abiding Wonder

This wonder in the earth may be hard for some to fathom. But as I mentioned before, the very minute you begin to apply human intellect to understand supernatural manifestations, you are sure to fail. The carnal mind cannot understand the things of the spirit. Not only that, but the carnal mind is often rooted in doubt and even fueled by Satan himself. We see this clearly in Scripture when Jesus rebukes Peter, saying, "Get behind me, Satan! You are a hindrance to me. For you are not setting your mind on the things of God, but on the things of man" (Matt. 16:23). With that being said, do all things with the mind of Christ, remaining indwelt by the Spirit who knows all things, and you'll do just fine.

It was Memorial Day when I ran into an unexpected wonder. That particular morning, during the 3 to 6 a.m. watch, the presence of God was very rich and exceptionally intimate. I didn't think anything of it as I continued my day. After a bit of running around, I returned to my house. It was now about 3 p.m., and I went to take a brief power nap, as I will often do in order to recharge from waking up at 3 a.m., before continuing the rest of the day. I pulled back the comforter and sheets on my bed to find a grape vine in the exact spot that I lie. Yep, you read that correctly—a grape vine. I was just like you, thinking, *What in the world?* and, *How did that get there?* With years of ongoing wonders intertwined through the journey of life in God, I have come to learn that there is just nothing He can't or won't do to get His message across to humankind.

One other thing that is so amazing about God is the creativity with which He performs signs and wonders. Each sign and every wonder seem to be nothing like each other. They are all so diverse in implication and manifestation. It's like God is so vast and creative by nature that He can't help but express His loving intentions to humankind through unmatchable means, time and time again. The wonders that He may cause to manifest can be so mind-boggling at times that you might say, "Certainly it won't get any more creative or wild than this!" only to find out that the next one is just as creative, if not more so.

This wonder bought immediate revelation—I knew what it was all about. One of my favorite passages in all of scripture is where Jesus refers to Himself as the vine.

I am the true vine, and my Father is the vinedresser. Every branch in me that does not bear fruit he takes away, and every branch that does bear fruit he prunes, that it may bear more fruit. Already you are clean because of the word that I have spoken to you. Abide in me, and I in you. As the branch cannot bear fruit by itself, unless it abides in the vine, neither can you, unless you abide in me. I am the vine; you are the branches. Whoever abides in me and I in him, he it is that bears much fruit, for apart from me you can do nothing. If anyone does not abide in me he is thrown away like a branch and withers; and the branches are gathered, thrown into the fire, and burned. If you abide in me, and my words abide in you, ask whatever you wish, and it will be done for you. By this my Father is glorified, that you bear much fruit and so prove to be my disciples. As the Father has loved me, so have I loved you. Abide in my love. If you keep my commandments, you will abide in my love, just as I have kept my Father's commandments and abide in his love. These things I have spoken to you, that my joy may be in you, and that your joy may be full (John 15:1-11).

As we see in these verses, Jesus is the vine, and intimate abiding within this vine is what bears much fruit. Jesus even goes on to say, "Abide in My love." This grape vine that was placed upon my bed was a clear wonder in the earth in direct parallel with this passage. He had strategically placed the vine upon my bed exactly where I lie in representation of intimacy and the need to abide within the vine of the Lord Jesus Christ. This was also why God chose Memorial Day to perform this sign—this was to be a commemoration of great value and therefore something to never forget. God was not negating the value of the true meaning of this holiday in our nation or what so many dear lives paid for our freedom. This is merely how God speaks within the riddles and parables of life. And one thing I can assure you, my friend—if there is anything you need to hold so dear, never forget it is your daily abiding in the vine of one true love.

Prayer

God, I thank You for Your wonders in the earth. Speak to us, I pray, through the performance of Your signs. Communicate with us through the manifestation of Your wondrous deeds. Increase our capability to understand Your ways and voice. We love You; have Your way in and through our lives, we pray, from now till forevermore.

Chapter 6

GLORY WONDERS

IN THIS CHAPTER I WILL BE EMPHASIZING SIGNS AND WONDERS that come directly out of the presence and glory of God. What is so amazing about these wonders is that they typically manifest in times of adoration and worship. They tend to culminate out of the very presence of who He is. Intimacy is one of the key factors that plays into what I like to call *glory wonders*.

The Cloud of God's Glory

In Scripture, a literal cloud manifested from the glory of the Lord, "And when the priests came out of the Holy Place, *a cloud filled the house of the Lord*, so that the priests could not stand to minister because of the cloud, for the glory of the Lord filled the house of the Lord" (1 Kings 8:10-11). Oh, that we would return to the days of God's presence at this level, when ministers would not even be able to stand up under the weighty presence and glory of God. As if the appearance of a supernatural cloud wasn't profound enough, the literal, tangible presence of the glory of God was so densely manifested that humankind could not even stand up under its weighty magnificence.

The Cloud of Face-to-Face Communication

> *When Moses entered the tent, the pillar of cloud would descend and stand at the entrance of the tent, and the Lord would speak with Moses. And when all the people saw the pillar of cloud standing at the entrance of the tent, all the people would rise up and worship, each at his tent door. Thus the Lord used to speak to Moses face to face, as a man speaks to his friend* (Exodus 33:9-11).

This is probably my favorite sign and wonder in connection with the glory of God, simply because of what it represents—face-to-face communication, God speaking to humankind as He would to a friend. If that right there isn't the highest goal in life outside of marital union with Jesus Christ, I don't know what is.

Radiance of Glory

While we are speaking of glory wonders in correlation with Moses and his unprecedented face-to-face relations with God, Exodus 34 contains what is probably my second most favorite sign and wonder. Again, what makes this one so special is that this profound occurrence likewise follows communication with God.

> *When Moses came down from Mount Sinai, with the two tablets of the testimony in his hand as he came down from the mountain, Moses did not know that the skin of his face shone because he had been talking with God* (Exodus 34:29).

Moses was so in tune with the radiance of God's glory, presence, and voice that his skin literally took on that same illuminating effect. So much so that he had to physically put on a veil so the people could come near enough to hear what God had said. We see this same incident occur when Jesus was enveloped by the glory of God on the Mount of Transfiguration—before communing with whom? Oh, how interesting! Moses! And Elijah. Isn't it interesting that the only other figure from Scripture who we know was illuminated by the glory of God is one of the witnesses to appear when the same thing happened to Jesus?

The one difference is, the Bible says that Jesus' countenance was altered and His clothes became dazzling white. If it means what it says, that means Jesus' facial features literally transformed while His clothing became illuminating white in the visible cloud of glory. I tell you, nothing can transform like the presence and glory of God. As David prayed—oh, that we might dwell in it all the days of our lives.

Miracle Wonder in God's Glory

I was ministering in a conference at a precious church up in Hamilton, Montana. It was such a powerful time. We were seeing signs and wonders of all sorts—feathers, gold, and other glorious displays of His presence. One profound wonder that really stuck out to the pastor and me was a result of a miracle released from the presence and glory of God. I got up to preach directly after worship while the glory of God was still very thick and began to prophesy that miracles would begin to break out within the house from the raw presence and glory of God alone, without anybody even laying hands on them. The pastor later shared how when he heard this word, he thought, "Well, that's a good word...I can see that starting to happen in about a year or so." He was just being honest with where his faith was at for the time being. Lo and behold, that very night a man's deaf ears just popped open all by themselves—without anyone laying hands on him—from the thick presence and glory of God. The pastor later shared the testimony and explained that the Lord was speaking through this miracle and wonder of glory. God was speaking to his church about having their ears of the spirit opened to hear what the Spirit of God would say, and this was actually happening upon the release of this sign.

This is another key to how God's speaks through signs and wonders in healings and miracles. If you notice a certain emphasis upon similar healings and miracles happening within a service or meeting, often the message is in the display. As this pastor figured out, you might be seeing deaf ears opening up because God is releasing ears to hear in the spirit. Or another example would be if you are seeing blind eyes being opened as the overriding miracle of the night, this would be a sign of the church's eyes to see in the spirit being enlightened with great revelation to come.

Smoke of God's Wonder

Another quite astounding wonder from God's glory happened in a meeting where smoke actually came into the meeting. This happened in back to back conferences that were not even in the same city. The first conference it happened in, I was sitting in worship when this white feather just appeared out of nowhere on my stomach at 8:04 p.m. I grabbed it off of my shirt, stuck it in my Bible, and marked the time. (See fig. K in Appendix.)

This is one absolute "must" when it comes to tracking the voice of God through signs and wonders. He does not just do things out of happenstance. He does not just pick random times to release His glorious wonders within the earth. If it is God and His authentic wondrous display, you better believe it is with great intent and strategic measure. He is extremely precise in all that He does.

After tucking away the feather, I got up to preach. There was such a thick presence of God in the place that it was so easy to preach. The anointing was on a paramount scale in this meeting. I preached, we laid hands on the sick, and miracles broke out. Later, many people came up to me saying, "Did you smell that?"

And I asked, "Smell what?"

They replied, "Are you kidding me? You couldn't smell the smoke?" I had preached the whole service and never smelled a thing, while many people across the congregation, sitting in different locations, had smelled this strong smoke fragrance come through the sanctuary. The feather manifesting upon my shirt at 8:04 p.m. now made sense! This was in correlation with Revelation 8:4, "And the *smoke of the incense*, with the prayers of the saints, rose before God from the hand of the angel." This was a sign within a sign. The feather obviously represented angelic involvement—"the hand of the angel." It was resting upon my belly—the placement of one's spirit, as Jesus said, "out of his belly shall flow rivers of living water," referring to the Holy Spirit (see John 7:38 KJV). So, out of our spirit come prayers, and in this case, the prayers of the saints in Revelation 8:4, which rise like smoke and incense before the throne of God.

This was a profound sign of the end times, as Revelation 8:4 occurs right before the last and final trumpets are blown. It also had local meaning—what God was doing within this church body. His desire was for a greater increase of prayer to begin within this church and the Body of Christ. This is another thing about God you will notice with signs and wonders. He will intertwine meanings for now and then, here and there, and broad and narrow, all at once. He is so multifaceted that He can speak two things out of one message. Psalm 62 refers to this: "One thing God has spoken, two things I have heard" (Ps. 62:11 NIV).

Following this event, we moved on to the next conference. I preached again, and we had an amazing time of His presence coming and wonders breaking out followed by the smell of smoke! I thought, *Amazing! What is going on here?* The very next morning I got up to pray after the late meeting the night before. When I stepped over to the coffee machine, a feather appeared in midair, right in front of my belly, and began floating up before me. I caught it, checked the time—and yep, you guessed it, 8:04. It was Revelation 8:4 again—the prayers of the saints (from the belly/spirit) going up like *smoke* before the throne by the hand of the angel (the feather). This sign followed the meeting to once again explain why the smoke sensation had returned. God was doing it again, getting His message across to not only this local body, but also the Body of Christ at large with the end-time implication before the last and final trumpet.

Wonders of Oil

On several occasions we have seen the amazing wonder of God's glory in the manifestation of oil. Oil speaks of the anointing of God and the Holy Spirit. Psalm 23 says, "You anoint my head with oil; my cup overflows" (Ps. 23:5). First Samuel 10:1 says, "Then Samuel took a flask of oil and poured it on his head and kissed him and said, 'Has not the Lord anointed you to be prince over his people Israel?'" This was followed by a great rushing of the Holy Spirit upon Saul. In Isaiah 61 we see where the Holy Spirit is linked to the "oil of joy" (Isa. 61:3 NKJV). As you can see, where the Holy Spirit of God is, you have the presence of oil, and the same goes for the anointing of God.

One of the most amazing times I've seen the oil of God manifest in His presence and glory was in a conference I was speaking at in Whitefish, Montana. The first night that it happened, this lady came up to me after I had preached and showed me this oil just oozing out of her hands. It was quite a profound sight. Both palms, including all fingers, were covered in oil. She said she was a worshiper and this happens in the glory of God. The next time I preached in that conference, I began to talk about the supernatural realities of God along with divine encounter, and the oil began to flow from her hands once more. It was such an astounding wonder of God's glory, and a manifestation of the anointing and Holy Spirit resting upon this woman's life.

Another mind-boggling wonder of oil occurred one night when I came out of a profound dream that God had given me, foreseeing a dire need to come. I woke up out of this dream around 1:22 a.m. and looked over to notice this manifestation of oil all over the cover of my journal. This journal is one that I compiled some time back to help people begin to steward God's voice. The title of the journal is *Stewarding the Mysteries of God*, and it is all about stewarding God's voice through dreams and visions. Well lo and behold, I had just come out of one of the most profound dreams of my life as far as what it represented and what was to come. Now I had this full display of oil all over the cover of my journal.

What was more amazing than its appearance alone was that the oil appeared to be coming out of the open book pictured on the cover of the journal. You see, I worked with a graphic designer to come up with the cover to the journal. It pictures an open book with gold flakes, lights, and swirls of smoke coming out of it, representing God's mysteries and wonders opening up to us by revelation, which we are to carefully steward. First Corinthians 4:1 says we are to regard ourselves as *stewards* of the mysteries of God. That's exactly what this journal was created for and represents—stewarding, tracking, and interpreting the voice and mysteries of God.

So this oil was now literally starting at the opening of the book image on this journal cover and just exploding up into the "mysteries of God" represented in the image. There was even more to this sign and wonder of oil because it hinged around such a significant dream. The dream happened on 2/22 of the Hebrew calendar, parallel with Daniel 2:22 and God's mysteries and revelations that this journal represented stewarding. That very same day, some random person donated $222 to our ministry. I just kept getting more spiritual parallels and implications to this sign about recording and tracking the voice of God in our lives. It was once again a wonder of God's anointing and Holy Spirit resting upon that which He cares so dearly about—communication and intimacy with His loving creation, you and I.

The Wonder of Bearing His Wounds

Many people are not aware of this, but bearing the wounds and marks of Jesus Christ is an actual sign and wonder. It is referred to as the *stigma*, or in plural form *stigmata*. By definition it means to be branded or marked. In this wonder, certain followers of Jesus Christ will literally take on the Lord's wounds and/or pain of the physical persecution He went through as a sign. This is prophetic of an experiential relationship with Him. This profound wonder has been happening all throughout the ages, well-documented and recorded, to everyone's amazement time and time again.

Often people read right over the first recorded stigmatist in Scripture—the apostle Paul. In Galatians 6:17 he states very clearly, "From now on let no one cause me trouble, for I bear on my body *the marks of Jesus*." These were not marks received because of the Lord Jesus. These were not persecuted marks from being beat for the gospel, although Paul certainly received his share of those as well. It is what it says—*the marks of Jesus*, period. This is a profound wonder that many are not even aware exists, but nevertheless it has been well documented throughout the ages.

I would go on to say that this is one of the most profound wonders in all of creation by the implications alone. There is no feat in all of history greater than what the Lord Jesus did for us when He was crucified for the salvation of the world. There was no greater task than laying down His life for you and I that we might live. This manifested sign has been entrusted to so few throughout history. It is a reminder and a small token that we at times are privileged to share in His sufferings as we also take up our cross daily and commune with Him in the life of death and resurrection power. I don't think it could have been any more well put than how Paul spoke of it, "That I may know him and the power of his resurrection, and may share his sufferings, becoming like him in his death" (Phil. 3:10).

On several occasions, I have been so graced to have encounters that tied directly in to the Lord's passion and our sharing in that suffering as believers. One time, I was awakened out of a dead sleep in the middle of the night about 1 a.m. My right arm had been pulled out to the side as if to be nailed to the cross, just like the crucifixion. I felt a sharp pain pierce through my right palm, exactly where the nails would have pierced the Lord Jesus Christ. The pain remained for about half of an hour, then dissipated. I thought, *What on earth was that all about?* The very next day I found out that a fellow graduate from the Bible school I attended had been martyred halfway across the world—at the very hour that I was having the experience. He was the first martyr our Bible college had ever sent out, and the Lord Jesus was allowing me to prophetically experience what was happening as this precious young man gave up his life for the cause of Christ. This young man was a pro-phetic parallel to what Jesus did on the cross of Calvary, sharing in the sufferings of the Lord Jesus Christ and giving up his life. I was merely given experiential insight into what was happening to this young man. The Lord was revealing that this sacrifice was worthy to be compared to the sufferings He endured. It reminds me of the verse about Jesus, "who for the joy that was set before him endured the cross" (Heb. 12:2).

Not long after this experience, I was scheduled to preach at a church for a three-day conference. The night before the last service, the exact same thing happened. My hands were pulled out in cruci-fied fashion, waking me out of a dead sleep at 12:39 a.m. The Lord spoke to me very clearly that this church was about to go through a six-month purging/cross-bearing season that would bring about great resurrection power. This was the prophetic meaning behind the experience happening at 12:39 a.m. The time of 12:39 repre-sented the 12th year, 3rd to 9th month. This crucified purging would span from the third month until the ninth month of 2012. Although these aren't always the happiest words to share, I've come to learn that you just say what the Lord tells you to say, nothing more and nothing less. The more obedient you remain in the walk of faith, the better off you will be, whether you make friends along the way or not. It is Him we all answer to one day, so I would advise you to make Him the only one you obey at the end of each day.

I shared the word, and thank Jesus it was well received. Fol-lowing the sermon, during ministry time, one of the most peculiar things I had ever seen happened. A lady came up to me astonished at what had taken place. During the service she had received a stigma in her right palm.

It was one of the wildest things I had ever beheld. There was literally an indentation of what would appear to be a spike wound right in the center of her palm. (See fig. L in Appendix.) It was a sign and wonder following the word of the crucified life, now displayed through this lady's palm. Later down the road, I ran into this precious woman of God again, and she still had the mark. As far as I know, it is still there to this day. God, that we may be found worthy to share in the sufferings of Jesus Christ and His resurrection power, that we may bring glory to Your name, and throughout the earth display Your fame.

Waiting Wonder

This next wonder that happened in the glory of God is one of my all-time favorites. It manifested as the famous verse says, "But they who wait for the Lord shall renew their strength; they shall mount up with wings like eagles; they shall run and not be weary; they shall walk and not faint" (Isa. 40:31).

I was waiting upon the Lord one morning, as I typically do from 3 to 6 a.m. In my first book, *Modern Day Mysticism*, I go into further detail as to why this three-hour watch has become so important. Scripture refers to 3 to 6 a.m. as the fourth watch and it has been, without a doubt, the most revelatory window of time in hearing and seeing the voice of God. You say, "Seeing the voice of God?" Yes, that is exactly what I said. Habakkuk 2 says, "I will climb my watchtower and wait to *see* what the Lord will tell me to say" (Hab. 2:1 GNT), and this is one of the primary ways in which God speaks to His children—through sight. For example—dreams, visions, and prophetic pictures.

So I was waiting upon the Lord in stillness and silence for this three-hour span, receiving multifaceted realms of revelation. Typically I will record what I see, hear, and experience in a journal or voice recorder. This morning I just so happened to be using a voice recorder. There was one small problem, though—the batteries in my voice recorder this particular morning were on their last leg. There is a battery power gauge on the screen of the voice recorder that reveals how much strength is left in your batteries. That way you don't get caught stranded with something of great importance to record but without sufficient power. The voice recorder takes normal AAA batteries. Nothing special. Not even rechargeable. Right around 6 a.m. I was concluding this prayer watch of waiting upon the Lord with Isaiah 40:31, "renew their strength." I grabbed the voice recorder to record one of the last things I had seen.

You're not going to believe what happened next—I couldn't believe it myself, although it happened right before my eyes. Just as I grabbed the voice recorder in my right hand, the battery gauge went from one last bar of power all the way up to full strength. It now read all bars with full strength, as if I had put brand new batteries in the recorder. I was blown away and knew immediately that it was a sign and wonder of Isaiah 40:31—a treasured verse that I hold so dear.

You see, many people tend to think that this verse, along with many others in the Bible, is a mere cliché or spiritual parallel of some sort. But I tell you, my friend, the Bible is way more literal than we often give it credit for. If the Bible says it, I believe it, and that's that. If it has spiritual implications as well—so be it, I'll take that too. But I certainly would not recommend spiritualizing everything, thereby diluting the possibilities of heaven operating within your midst.

So here it was—a full-blown sign and wonder in parallel with one of my all-time favorite verses in the Bible. Renewed strength due to waiting upon the Lord. And yes, it is one of my favorite Scriptures, because it has to do with spending time with Him. There is nothing of greater importance than spending time with

Him day in and day out. Never forget that, my friend. Intimacy is the highest call anyone can undertake.

And just think—if this happened as a sign in two AAA batteries after one three-hour watch of prayer, can you imagine what happens to our entire being when we are enveloped by His glory on a day-to-day basis? I tell you, my friend, there is no higher call than that of waiting upon the Lord and intimately getting to know Him. When you do, His manifest presence literally transforms and renews everything about you. You do not become refurbished, so to speak, but made brand new. We become regenerated by the divine life that proceeds from His throne. Isn't it awesome that we've been given this much access to commune with the King of the universe? We have the ability to be made brand new on a daily basis within His presence divine.

I can remember a season of prayer that I was in for about a year. I was praying for no less than nine hours per day. Often I would be in prayer for eleven, twelve, even up to sixteen hours per day. And one way Isaiah 40:31 became literally real to me in that time—I was only requiring around four to five hours of sleep per night. I was living out of such an overflow of Him who never sleeps nor slumbers and is filled with power and sovereign life that I no longer needed the rest that most people think we require. You see, His presence is rest. His presence is life. His presence is the life-giver of all things eternal. Wait upon the Lord and be made new.

Gold, Silver, and Precious Stones

Signs and wonders of gold, silver, and precious stones are other manifestations of God's being and voice in the realms of glory. A shimmering, dust-like deposit of gold and silver has been showing up for quite some time, and now appears in just about every meeting. Gold dust actually began to appear upon my hands as I started writing the angelic wonders chapter of this book. Angels also carry this shimmering substance, which is no doubt abundant in heaven, to us from the glory of God. And the stones and shimmering particles that we see are also mentioned throughout Scripture. One of those places is the foundational stones of heaven:

> *The foundations of the wall of the city were adorned with every kind of jewel. The first was jasper, the second sapphire, the third agate, the fourth emerald, the fifth onyx, the sixth carnelian, the seventh chrysolite, the eighth beryl, the ninth topaz, the tenth chrysoprase, the eleventh jacinth, the twelfth amethyst* (Revelation 21:19-20).

Alongside the regular manifestation of gold and silver, I've been so honored to see the sapphire, the emerald, and the onyx in glorious manifestations of His expression and voice.

One time while in prayer I got taken into a vision where I saw the Lord Jesus open up a Bible and blow into it. At this, sapphire dust came out of the Bible and onto me. Several days following, this very same shimmering sapphire dust appeared upon my face. This was a sign and wonder in God's glory. Jesus was opening up greater revelation to me. Blue represents revelation, and opening up the word and breathing it upon me was obviously the breath of the Spirit behind the revelation to come. So in this case I saw a vision, which was soon confirmed by a sign and wonder.

I have learned, with the realm of the eternal, that if you can see it on that side, you can have it on this side. If you break it open through the eternal, you can access it through the temporal. You see, heaven is obviously the superior realm, and if you can obtain that which you desire on that side you can release it on this side. This falls in line with the famous verse, "Whatever you bind on earth shall be bound in heaven, and whatever you loose on earth shall be loosed in heaven" (Matt. 16:19). It's just mere protocol. Handle your business in the superior realm (heaven), and it will take care of itself in the inferior realm (earth).

Another time, this precious man of God prayed for an impartation of signs and wonders over me. We were at a conference, and the meeting was about to begin. Immediately following the prayer I went into worship. With my eyes closed, I felt a strong gust of wind blow past the right side of my body. I thought, *Surely someone just ran by me.* I looked, and no one was there. I thought, *Okay, there must be a fan or air conditioning vent overhead.* I looked up and found nothing. The only thing I did end up finding was gold and onyx dust all over my right hand—the side of my body the wind had blown by. This was a sign and wonder of the apostolic impartation that this minister carried and was now releasing upon my life:

> *They made the onyx stones, enclosed in settings of gold filigree, and engraved like the engravings of a signet, according to the names of the sons of Israel. And he set them on the shoulder pieces of the ephod to be stones of remembrance for the sons of Israel, as the Lord had commanded Moses* (Exodus 39:6-7).

When you see onyx and gold manifested together, it definitely represents the apostolic. As we saw in Exodus 39, there were onyx stones set in gold filigree and placed upon the shoulder pieces of the ephod. Shoulders always represent the governmental apostolic role in the church. And if you read further, each stone bore the name of one of the tribes of Israel—twelve stones in total. Twelve is also the key number representing the apostolic ministry; Jesus selected the twelve apostles in line with God's methods and numerology.

Another wondrous manifestation of God's glory came in a season of my life when I was in dire need of God's word on a crucial subject in my life. About that time, I was attending a conference in Dallas, Texas. I ended up attending this conference annually for many years. This was one of the main conferences in which I experienced the falcon encounter that I referred to earlier. This particular year at this conference, God finally spoke to me clearly about how the future would unfold for this crucial topic. I left thrilled and gladdened by the new revelation God had given. Would you believe that exactly one year later at the exact same conference a diamond appeared at my feet, confirming the prior year's promise?

Diamonds represent promise and covenant, and the Lord was following the previous year with a sign to confirm what He had spoken to me the year prior in the exact same place. It amazes me how He waited for the anniversary and exact geographical location of the given word to release the confirming sign one year later. He is so intricate when it comes to displaying His love for us. That which He spoke did come to pass, by the way. If He says it, it will happen. If He promises something to you, it is certain to fulfill itself. The only one who can stop His promises from coming to pass is you. The Israelites did it in the wilderness. They turned a small journey into 40 years and still never saw the Promised Land. Although His promises are true, they are conditional at the same time. You are not going to live a life of disobedience and see the promises of God culminate in your life, my friend. Obey and walk out His highest plan or disobey and miss out on the greater things He had in store for you.

Gold of First Love

This wonder of God's glory goes down in my books as one of the most special, because it relates to returning to the first love of relationship with Him.

I was in Los Angeles, preparing to minister at a Korean house of prayer. The night before ministering at this house of prayer, an angel came and brushed my forehead at 2:35 a.m., waking me out of a dead sleep. This has happened many times now, and I have learned that the angel brushes my forehead as a sign of foreknowing. The head, where our brain is, represents thoughts, and the forehead has come to represent foreknowledge.

For example, I was ministering in Chicago, Illinois when an angel came and brushed my forehead at 10:38 p.m. I knew immediately that this meant Acts 10:38, "Jesus…went about doing good and healing all who were oppressed by the devil." This gave me foreknowledge to direct the service. With Acts 10:38 being one of the most paramount healing verses in all of the Bible, I knew to direct the service and especially ministry time around healings and miracles. Sure enough, in this smaller congregation we had a deaf ear open up and several other healings, to God's glory. I woke up the next day and learned one small, extra wild detail about this revelation—the very Internet domain name of the place I was staying while in Chicago was *Acts 10:38!*

I was blown away, but it once again shows the intricacy behind everything God does and orders, if we pay attention and follow Him to the best of our ability. I've even had an angel tap me on the side of my head—my temple—before a service at 12:34, revealing divine order and alignment within the house of God. The temple represented the "temple" or house of God, and 12:34 meant that God was applying His divine alignment within the church—1, 2,

3, 4 being the "correct order." You see, if you begin to slow down, wait upon the Lord, and pray for the Spirit of wisdom and revelation to increase upon your life, a whole new dimension of His voice will open up to you and enlighten you to how often He has been speaking all along. Most often, it's not that He's not speaking, but that we aren't hearing.

Back to the story of the Korean house of prayer. The Lord revealed to me that the angel brushing my forehead at 2:35 was in direct parallel with Revelation 2:3-5.

> *I know you are enduring patiently and bearing up for my name's sake, and you have not grown weary. But I have this against you, that you have abandoned the love you had at first. Remember therefore from where you have fallen; repent, and do the works you did at first* (Revelation 2:3-5).

I thought, *No way! This can't be!* Koreans are very devout people by nature, and when they are committed to something there is no question of the level of their commitment—it's wholehearted. But as I mentioned earlier, when the Lord gives you something to say— especially when He sends an angel to deliver the message—you are better off telling it just like it is. So the following day came, and I was greatly honored to be with these precious believers of Korean descent. The worship was very passionate and lasted almost two hours. If you had looked upon the outside, you would have never seen any sign of forsaking their first love in any form or fashion. But I preached it anyway, exactly out of Revelation 2:3-5, and what followed was absolutely astonishing.

A precious young woman of God came up at the end, and to everyone's amazement she was covered in gold dust. It was everywhere. All over her blouse, all down her arms, all over her pants, and even down the back of her pants. I haven't a clue how that happened—she was sitting in a chair for most of the preaching—but when God wants to display His wonders, material objects do not seem to get in His way. So the young woman was covered in gold, and I asked her what happened. She said, "You are not going to believe this, but about a month ago I had a dream that this man in a blue shirt came up to me telling me to return to my first love. Then he started telling me details about my life that only God knew, and I then came out of the dream." Would you believe that the color of the shirt I happened to wear that night was blue?

Here it was, a sign of God's golden glory covering this precious woman of God as she was called back to her first love. It had even been foreshown to her a month before in a prophetic dream. She and many others in the meeting, including the leader, later confessed that it was true—they had forsaken their first love very subtly over time by putting more focus on careers and life paths than the intimate pursuit of loving and knowing Him. God is so good! What was also so amazing about this incident was that this precious young woman had never experienced gold dust as a wonder from the presence and glory of God, but she had heard of it before and desired to experience it. And God lovingly wooed her back to loving relationship with Him and gave her the desire of her heart in this wonder.

We have seen this shimmering dust appear in many different instances for many different purposes. I'm reminded of one young lady whom this glory dust appeared upon. Ever since, she has been going into astounding visions with revelation following. Another person had this gold appear on their hands for two days. Their hands got hot in the meeting, representing the healing anointing, and then became covered in gold. Following this, they couldn't seem to make the shimmering presence and glory of God go away.

I've seen this shimmering wonder come upon people who paralleled Scripture when the verse was preached from the pulpit. The methods God uses to perform these wonders are endless. He is way too vast and creative to be confined to one or two outlets of communication. Be open, my friend, and remain passionately in love as He leads you down this unmatchable journey of knowing Him.

Prayer

God, I thank You for the vast array of glorious wonders that manifest from Your throne. I thank You that Your presence and glory are the foundation by which all things live. Release Your wonders from the realms of glory like we've never seen before in this day and age. Be glorified in and through Your church by the message-riddled sign and the awestruck wonder. Let the Spirit of wisdom and revelation be released to assist, I pray, that we might be enlightened in understanding the work of Your hands.

Chapter 7

THE GREATEST SIGN AND WONDER OF ALL—JESUS

HANDS DOWN, IN ALL OF HISTORY AND THROUGHOUT ALL OF creation, the greatest sign and wonder there ever was or ever will be is none other than Jesus Christ. He is the King of kings and Lord of lords, the Prince of Peace, the Alpha and Omega, the Bread of Life, the Bright and Morning Star, the Chosen One, the Chief Cornerstone, the Bridegroom who was and is to come. His birth, entire life, and culminating death was without a doubt the greatest sign and wonder of all time. There never has been nor ever will be a greater expression of God to man. All of who God is was entirely wrapped up into the flawless Lamb who was slain. Every step that He took and every movement that He made fulfilled the precise directions of the Father. His very life lived out was the most prolific sign and wonder that creation will ever know. One could spend eternity studying His life through the gospels and merely be scratching the surface of what it fully expressed—Jesus, the same yesterday, today, and forever, the greatest wonder of all.

Everything Pointed to Jesus

Everything before Jesus pointed ahead. Everything after Him pointed behind. This one thing you can be sure of, my friend:

No matter in history where you look and begin,
it all points to Him from beginning to end.

Before the cross, after the cross, whenever you
choose. Missing the Son? You are certain to lose.

You can rewind, fast-forward, or pause all the same,
and all you will find is His due glory and fame.

Counselor, Good Shepherd, Victorious One,
He's God's gift to us, in comparison to none.

Quencher of all thirst and manna divine, the
Light of the world enabling all to then find.

The gateway to heaven, salvation through none
other than Jesus, God's only begotten Son.

He's the focal point, throughout whom all lives should
live, to Him in return our whole hearts we must give.

No matter the amazement of historic feats
that stand tall, Jesus will always remain
the greatest sign and wonder of all.

Old Testament Wonders of Jesus

The entire Old Testament was riddled with signs and wonders that foreshadowed the soon-coming King. When Moses struck the rock so that water came out and supplied drink for the children of God, it was a direct parallel to the crucified Christ. Not only did Jesus refer to Himself as the water that would quench eternal thirst (see John 4:14), but He was struck in the side and water came out along with the blood (see John 19:34). This represented the salvation of the world and the eternal fountain of life to sustain all of humankind.

The manna that came down in the wilderness as provision for the Israelites was another wonder which reflected the Son of Man. In John 6, Jesus went on to say, "I am the bread that came down from heaven" (John 6:41), referring to Himself as the Bread of Life. He is the source of all sufficiency in the wilderness of life. This sign, which kept the children of God alive, was a natural wonder that paralleled salvation—the Savior of the world, and the eternal destination of humankind.

As I mentioned earlier, Jonah in the belly of the whale was another lived-out wonder—a sign of Jesus in the grave for three days and three nights. Jesus even confirmed this to be a sign of Himself:

> But no sign will be given to it except the sign of the prophet Jonah. For just as Jonah was three days and three nights in the belly of the great fish, so will the Son of Man be three days and three nights in the heart of the earth (Matthew 12:39-40).

The blood of the lamb upon the doorposts in Exodus represented the Lamb of God who would take away the sin of the world.

On top of the biblical parallels that foreshadowed His coming, there were over 300 Old Testament prophecies that declared the details of His birth, life, death, and resurrection. By the way, these were complete signs and wonders in and of themselves. All of Scripture is riddled with accounts that profess the soon-coming King.

His Birth, Life, Death, and Ascension

The very birth, life, death, and resurrected ascension of the Lord Jesus Christ were all unmatchable wonders of His glory and fame. His birth alone was virginal, as we all know, which is clearly impossible without the working of God. He was the very seed/offspring of God imparted to humankind. He was birthed into a world of sin from a place of knowing no sin, so that He might redeem it from the state into which it had fallen.

Jesus then lived out a complete life of 33 years in the midst of all-out corruption and persecution without one spot or blemish of the world tainting His flawless life of upright perfection. The only thing that was affected was the darkness around Him. This is what I love about Jesus so much—everywhere He goes and everything He does, He is the standard, and everything changes according to Him. He is never swayed or changed or moved by anything but the will of His Father. You will either follow Him or choose your eternal demise.

His death was the greatest sign and wonder throughout all of history, allowing humankind access to the Father. As His flawless blood poured out upon His last breath, making the one and only gateway to heaven, the earth shook, saints resurrected, rocks were split, and the temple veil completely tore in two. The centurion and company were lead to immediate conversion upon seeing the earthquake:

> And behold, the curtain of the temple was torn in two,
> from top to bottom. And the earth shook, and the rocks

were split. The tombs also were opened. And many bodies of the saints who had fallen asleep were raised, and coming out of the tombs after his resurrection they went into the holy city and appeared to many. When the centurion and those who were with him, keeping watch over Jesus, saw the earthquake and what took place, they were filled with awe and said, "Truly this was the Son of God" (Matthew 27:51-54).

His third-day resurrection was a complete wonder; He overcame death and hell so all of humanity might know and experience His victory. Jesus made this very clear, "Fear not, I am the first and the last, and the living one. I died, and behold I am alive forevermore, and I have the keys of Death and Hades" (Rev. 1:18). Paul also alludes to this triumphant defeat, "O death, where is your victory? O death, where is your sting?" (1 Cor. 15:55). The sting of death is sin, and the power of sin is the law. But thanks be to God, who gives us the victory through our Lord Jesus Christ.

The ascension of Jesus was the first recorded levitation in all of history, taking Him right into heaven.

And when he had said these things, as they were looking on, He was lifted up, and a cloud took him out of their sight. And while they were gazing into heaven as He went, behold, two men stood by them in white robes, and said, "Men of Galilee, why do you stand looking into heaven? This Jesus, who was taken up from you into heaven, will come in the same way as you saw Him go into heaven" (Acts 1:9-11).

His departure was even a sign of how He would return for the last and final time:

For the Lord himself will descend from heaven with a cry of command, with the voice of an archangel, and with the sound of the trumpet of God. And the dead in Christ will rise first. Then we who are alive, who are left, will be caught up together with them in the clouds to meet the Lord in the air, and so we will always be with the Lord (1 Thessalonians 4:16-17).

Jesus' Life Wonders

You had to watch everything Jesus did, as every move He made and action He took was with great mystery and wonder. Everything He did was a sign and had greater meaning than what was merely seen on the outside. It was like His entire life was this great treasure chest of mystery and revelation. The more you look into it, the greater the riches you will discover.

For example, when Jesus multiplied the loaves it was an astounding wonder accompanied by hidden mystery deep within. This was not only a wonder of great provision in the multiplication of food, but a sign that God's all sufficient government needed to remain void of the religious pollution in that day and age. You see, there is a deep mystery intertwined in what Jesus was discussing with the disciples and the numerical order He was showing them. When Jesus specifically asked them how many loaves were left over from each food multiplication, He was getting them to pronounce the answer—with a numerical prophetic message embedded within. We see this very clearly:

And he cautioned them, saying, "Watch out; beware of the leaven of the Pharisees and the leaven of Herod." And they began discussing with one another the fact that they had no bread. And Jesus, aware of this, said to them, "Why are you discussing the fact that you have no bread? Do you not yet perceive or understand? Are your hearts hardened? Having eyes do you not see, and having ears do you not hear? And do you not remember? When I broke the five loaves for the five thousand, how many baskets full of broken pieces did you take up?" They said to him, "Twelve." "And the seven for the four thousand, how many baskets full of broken pieces did you take up?" And they said to him, "Seven." And he said to them, "Do you not yet understand?" (Mark 18:15-21)

You have to pay very close attention here, or you will pass right over the deeper meaning Jesus was trying to get across. He started off by warning the disciples of the leaven of the Pharisees. This set the context of what Jesus talking about. While the disciples were still worried about natural means of provision and having no bread, Jesus continued to speak of purging the Pharisaical spirit. He said, "Do you still not understand?" and proceeded to ask them how many loaves were left over from the first food multiplication. He didn't ask how many fish were left over along with the loaves in this recreation miracle. He only spoke of the leftover loaves, as He was still speaking in the context of bread alone and the "leaven" of the Pharisees.

You see, He was far more concerned that His followers remained untainted by the religious spirit of the age than He was with their next meal. He was not even swayed by the immediate concern of not having any bread—it was a need easily met through the God who supplies all things. He was and is much more concerned with the spirit of the age polluting His work of building an eternal kingdom. In asking the disciples how many leftover loaves there were from Food Multiplication One and Food Multiplication Two, He got the answer He was looking for—twelve the first time and seven the second time. Jesus was thinking, *Precisely!* as He went on to ask, "Do you still not understand?"

You see, Jesus was not trying to get their response of how many baskets full were left over so they might have faith that He would provide. He was on an entirely different topic—abolishing the eternally destructive spirit of the Pharisees. He got the response He was looking for—the twelve and seven baskets of bread—and His message was within the numbers. Jesus said to beware of the spirit of the Pharisees, then followed with the point that "God's bread" multiplied, providing exactly twelve and seven baskets full left over as a sign. He then asked, "Do you still not understand?" He was getting at a deeper meaning—the number twelve represents the government of God and the number seven means "complete." Jesus' message in the sign was that God's all sufficient government is complete in and of itself, and must always remain free from the "leaven" of the Pharisaical spirit of that day.

Another one of my favorites was when Jesus cursed the fig tree. This was a not only a complete sign and wonder, it also had deep meaning hidden within. You will notice that Jesus cursed the fig tree, then cleansed the temple, then went back to the now-dead fig tree.

> *On the following day, when they came from Bethany, he was hungry. And seeing in the distance a fig tree in leaf, he went to see if he could find anything on it. When he came to it, he found nothing but leaves, for it was not the season for figs. And he said to it, "May no one ever eat fruit from you again." And his disciples heard it. And they came to Jerusalem. And he entered the temple and began to drive out those who sold and those who bought in the temple, and he overturned the*

tables of the money-changers and the seats of those who sold pigeons. And he would not allow anyone to carry anything through the temple. And he was teaching them and saying to them, "Is it not written, 'My house shall be called a house of prayer for all the nations'? But you have made it a den of robbers." And the chief priests and the scribes heard it and were seeking a way to destroy him, for they feared him, because all the crowd was astonished at his teaching. And when evening came they went out of the city. As they passed by in the morning, they saw the fig tree withered away to its roots (Mark 11:12-20).

Once again, Jesus strategically cursed the fig tree before cleansing the temple, then returned to the tree so that everyone could see the fig tree's fate. This was clearly another strategic wonder with greater meaning deep within. Jesus was not merely cursing the fig tree because it lacked fruit when He was hungry. The Bible says very clearly that it was not even the season for the tree to bear fruit. Jesus always did only what He saw the Father doing; He knew that He would be cleansing the temple, parallel with cursing the fig tree. He cursed the fig tree for not having fruit, cleansed the temple, and then showed the disciples how the fig tree was now dead.

Jesus knew that the religious leaders of that day were using the house of God for their personal gain, rather than devoting the house of God to prayer. This is the same Jesus who said, "Whoever abides in me and I in him, he it is that bears much fruit" (John 15:5). In other words, abiding in prayer in the house of God truly bears "fruit," which the fig tree and money exchangers were clearly not doing; for that, both received the curse/cleansing of Jesus, who was protecting the fruit of prayer. The cursing of the fig tree was nothing more than the mascot wonder, if you will, paralleling cleansing the temple. Neither were bearing fruit worthy of what was to come out of the House of God—prayer.

Jesus' life was full of these accounts—profound wonders intertwined with hidden messages and deep eternal insight. He turned the water into wine, walked on water during the fourth watch, paid taxes from the mouth of a fish, calmed the storm and raging sea—and the list goes on and on. His life was by far the greatest outplayed wonder in all of recorded history. There never has been anyone like Him and never will be throughout all of eternity. He is clearly the Son of God who came to take away the sins of the world.

If there is anything you ever do in this journey of knowing God's voice through signs and wonders, my friend, make sure there is one thing you never overlook—the life and person of the Man Jesus Christ. He is the greatest expression of God to man that you will every discover throughout eternity.

Let's Pray

God, I thank You for Your will, nature, and voice through signs and wonders. I thank You for greater understanding of how You move and operate and communicate through their demonstration. I ask even now that You would increase the outbreak of these mighty wonders within our lives, all for the purpose of knowing You and displaying Your glory in the earth.

And most of all I thank You for the greatest sign and wonder of all—Jesus. I ask above all things that we would get to know Jesus on a whole new level of deep intimate communion, becoming one with this Bridegroom King. I ask that we would be transformed into the very image of Jesus Christ and reflect You in this world for the transformation of humankind.

We love You, Father; we love You, Jesus; we love You, Holy Spirit. Release Your wonders, I pray. Release Your mighty signs. Let Your glory cover the earth as the water covers the sea.

OTHER BOOKS BY BRIAN GUERIN

Modern Day Mysticism

ABOUT BRIAN GUERIN

BRIAN GUERIN IS THE FOUNDER AND PRESIDENT OF BRIDAL GLORY International. He attended and graduated from the Brownsville School of Ministry/F.I.R.E. in 2001, and now travels throughout the US, as well as throughout the nations of the world, teaching and preaching the gospel of the Lord Jesus Christ. Brian has appeared as a guest on TBN, and also currently hosts his own broadcasting channel on XP Media. He has authored the book titled *Modern Day Mysticism* that has gone out all over the world, as well as the annual journal *Steward the Mysteries of God*. Brian's ministry is one of great prophetic precision, which literally facilitates heaven marked by unusual signs and wonders, powerful miracles and healings, accompanied by the very fingerprints of God. His number-one priority in life is hosting the Presence of God and walking in deep intimacy with the Bridegroom Jesus Christ while leading many to follow in this journey of greater depth in loving and knowing Him.

For more information or to contact Brian, go to:
Info@BridalGlory.com
www.bridalglory.com

APPENDIX

Many of these photos were taken with cell phones in order to capture the immediate occurrence; as such, the resolution is not professional quality.

fig. A

fig. B